M000282297

SPACE FRAMED

SPACE FRAMED

RICHARD GLUCKMAN ARCHITECT

ESSAY BY HAL FOSTER

First published in the United States of America in 2000
by The Monacelli Press, Inc.
10 East 92nd Street, New York, New York 10128

Copyright © 2000 The Monacelli Press, Inc.

All rights reserved under International and Pan-American Copyright
Conventions. No part of this book may be reproduced or utilized in
any form or by any means, electronic or mechanical, including
photocopying, recording, or by any information storage and retrieval
system, without permission in writing from the publisher. Inquiries
should be sent to The Monacelli Press, Inc.

Library of Congress Cataloging-in-Publication Data
Gluckman, Richard, 1947–
Space framed : Richard Gluckman architect / essay by Hal Foster.
p. cm.
Includes bibliographical references.
ISBN 1-58093-045-x (pb)
1. Gluckman, Richard, 1947– 2. Architecture, Modern—20th
century—New York (State)—New York. I. Title: Richard Gluckman
architect. II. Foster, Hal. III. Title.
NA737.G545 G58 2000
720'.92—dc21
99-098187

Printed in China

Design: Aline Ozkan, Michael Rock, 2x4 New York City

Front cover: Gagosian Gallery
Back cover: Paula Cooper Gallery

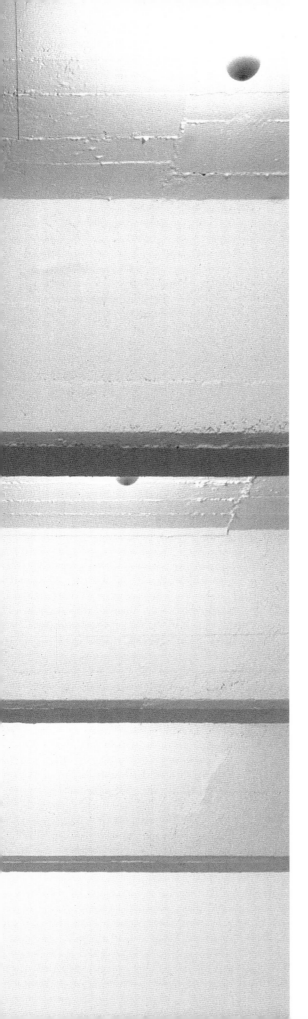

PROJECTS

01 | GLUCKMAN RESIDENCE 1968

03 | FRIEDRICH/DE MENIL RESIDENCE 1977

04|INSTALLATION FOR **THE NEW YORK EARTH ROOM**
BY WALTER DE MARIA 1979

05 | INSTALLATION FOR **THE BROKEN KILOMETER** BY WALTER DE MARIA 1980

EXIT

SELF-PORTRAITS

HERITAGE

HERITAGE

HERITAGE

11 | GORDON RESIDENCE 1990

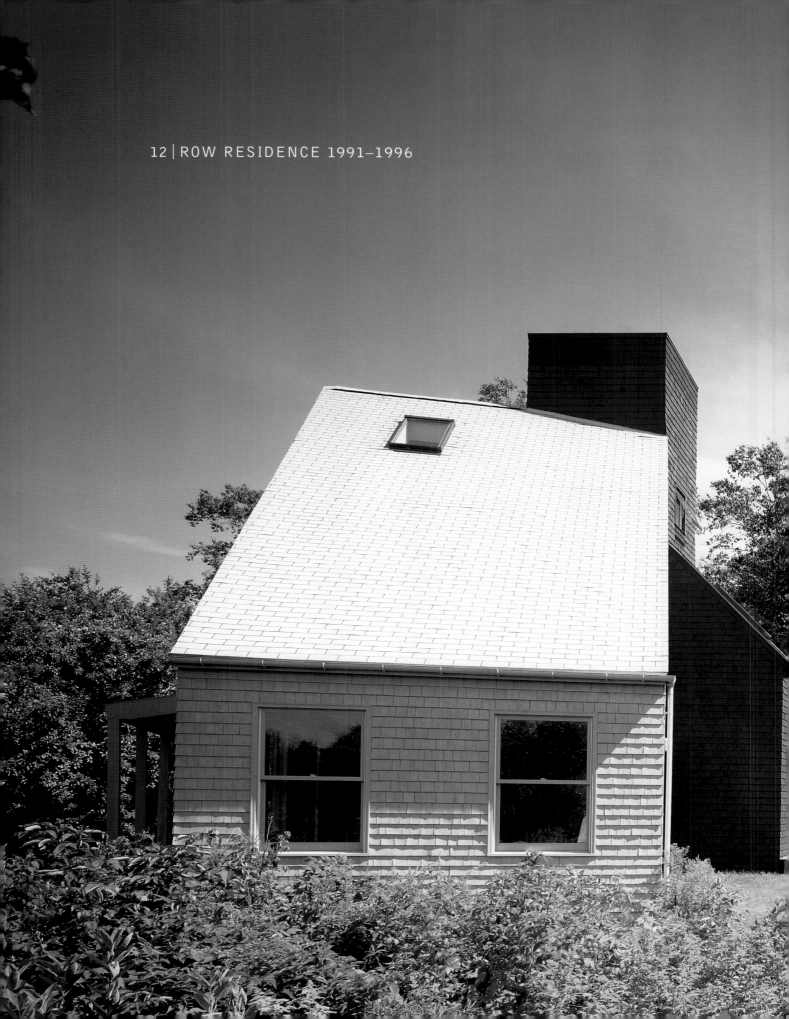

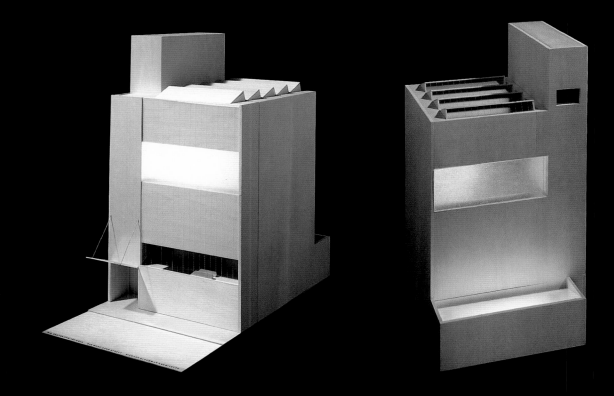

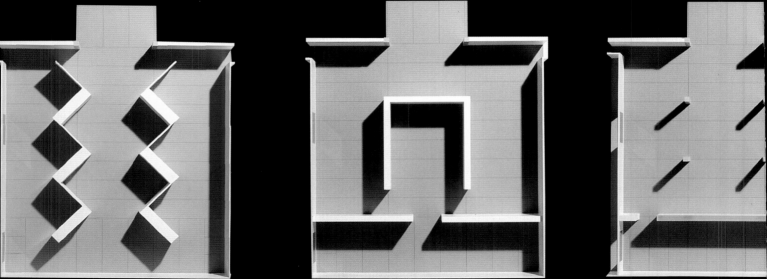

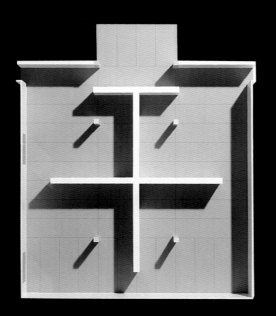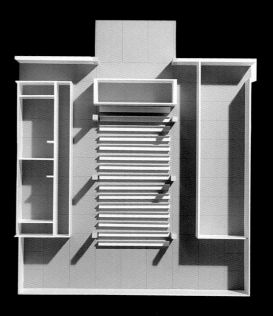

18 | INSTALLATION FOR **LUSTMORD** BY JENNY HOLZER 1994

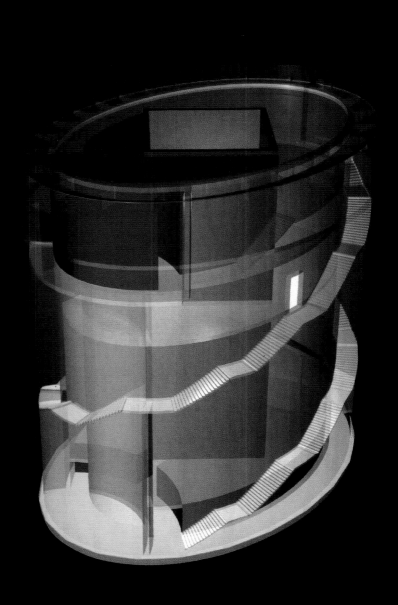

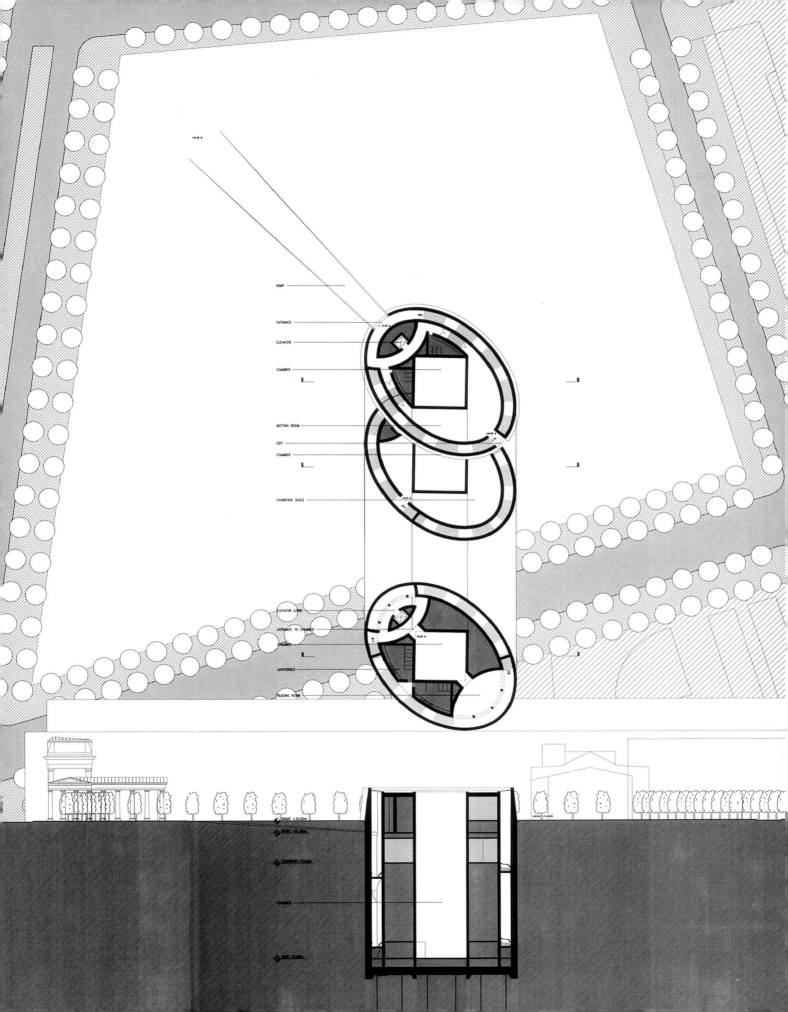

RAMP

ENTRANCE

ELEVATOR

CHAMBER

MEETING ROOM

EXIT

CHAMBER

EXHIBITION SPACE

ELEVATOR LOBBY

ENTRANCE TO CHAMBER

CHAMBER

LAVATORIES

READING ROOM

GRADE +34.00m

ENTRY +31.00m

EXHIBITION +27.00m

CHAMBER

BASE +4.00m

GRADE +34.00m

INFORMATION & MEMBERSHIP

JASPER JOHNS
18 OCTOBER 1977 · 22 JANUARY 1978
WHITNEY MUSEUM
OF AMERICAN ART

Whitney Museum of American Art
945 Madison Avenue New York

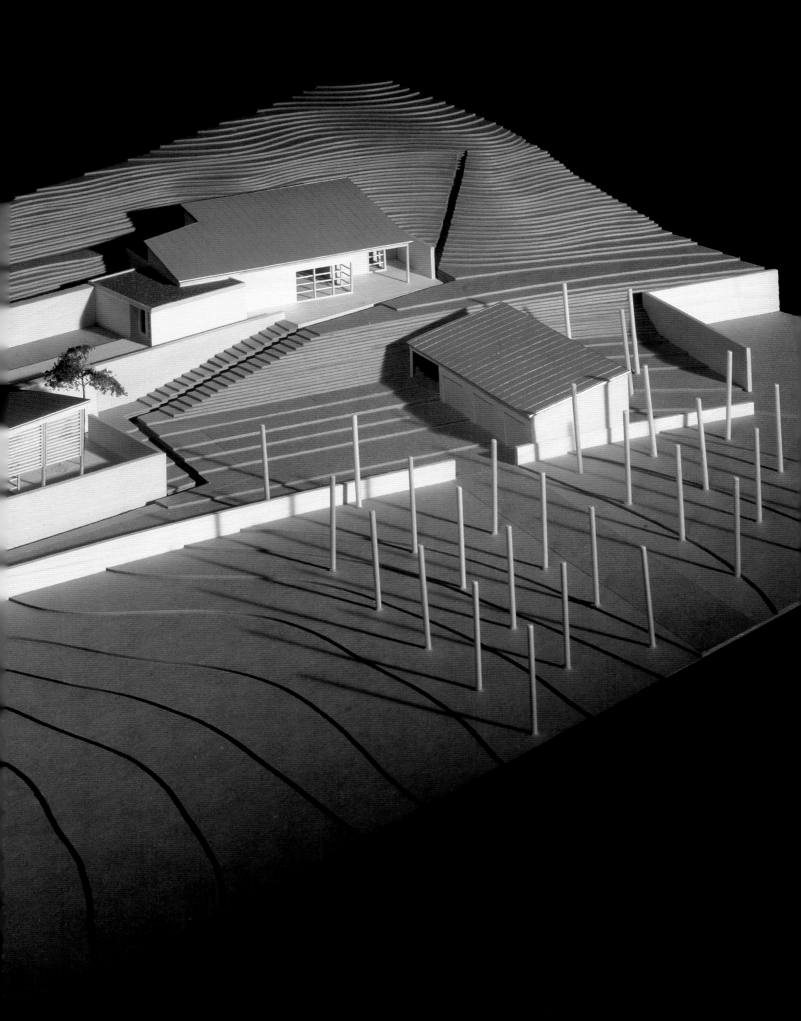

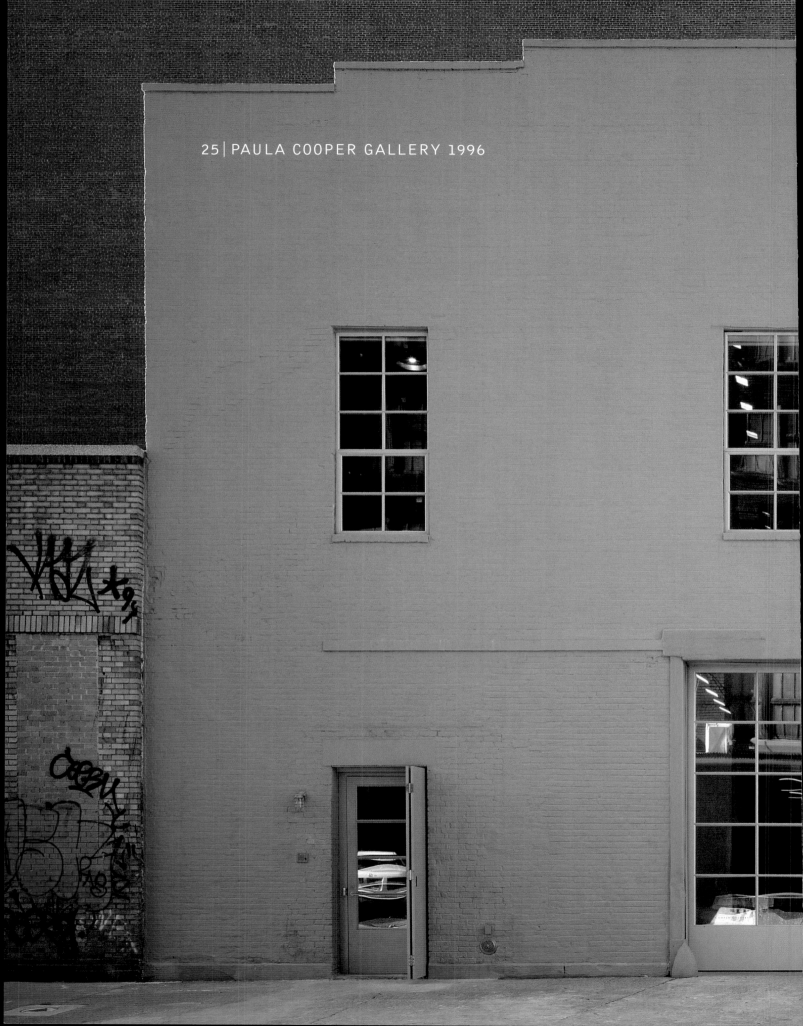

25 | PAULA COOPER GALLERY 1996

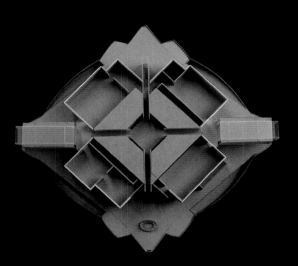

27 | GIANNI VERSACE BOUTIQUE 1998

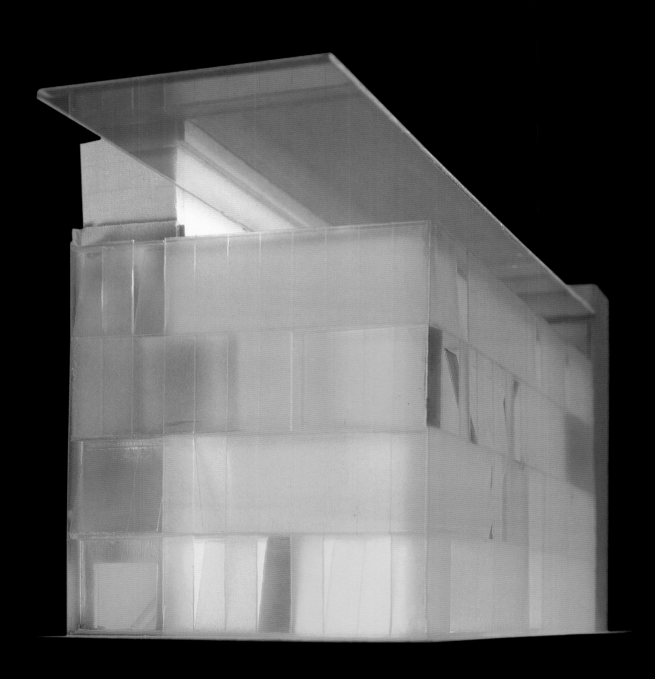

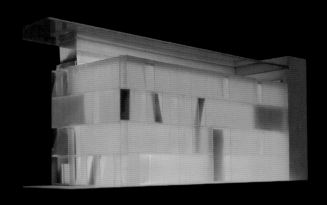

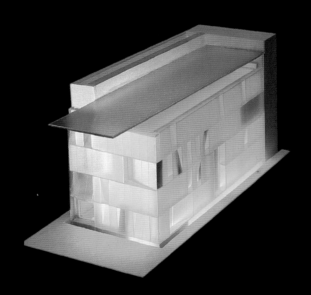

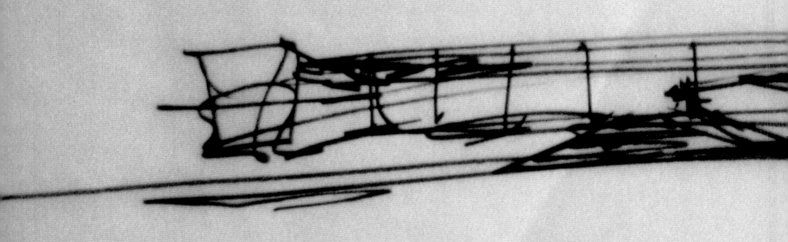

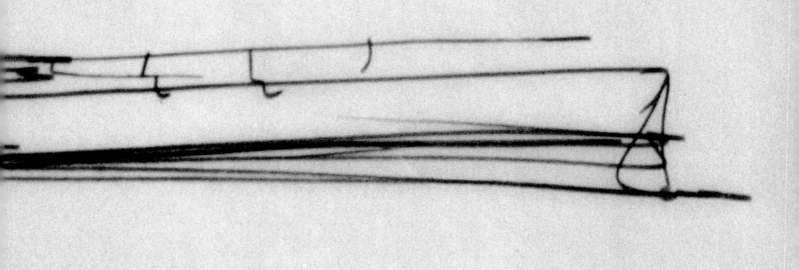

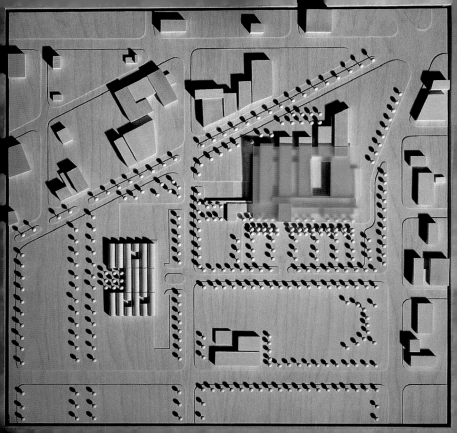

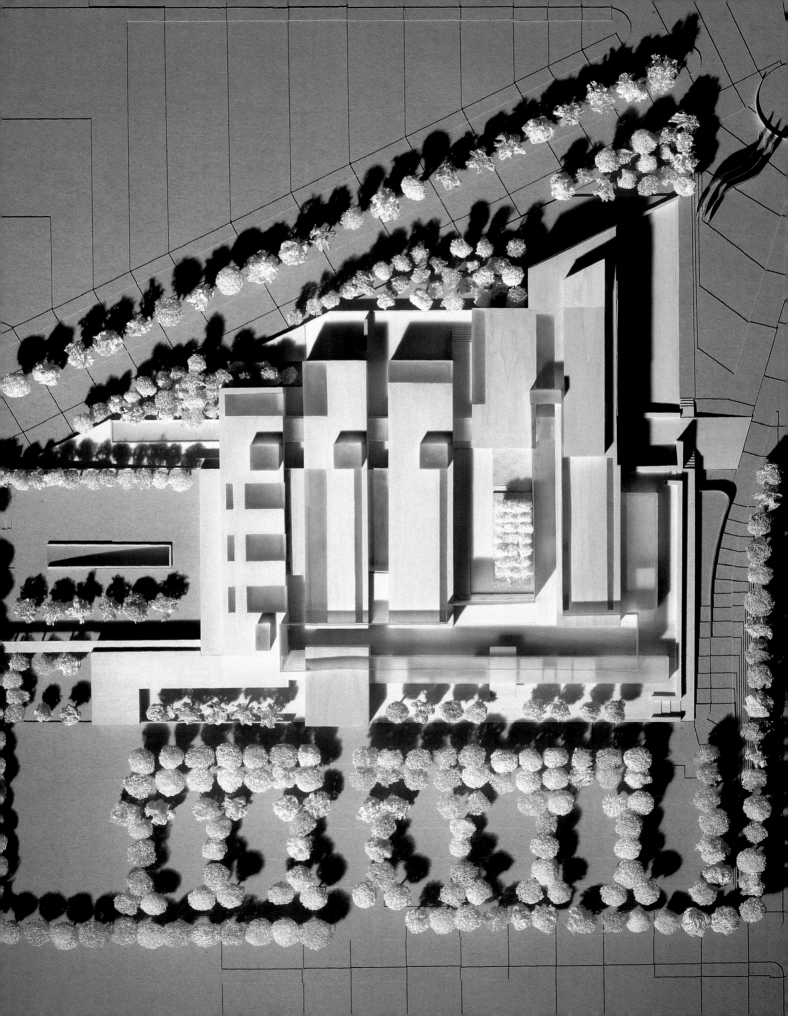

31 | GEORGIA O'KEEFFE MUSEUM 1997

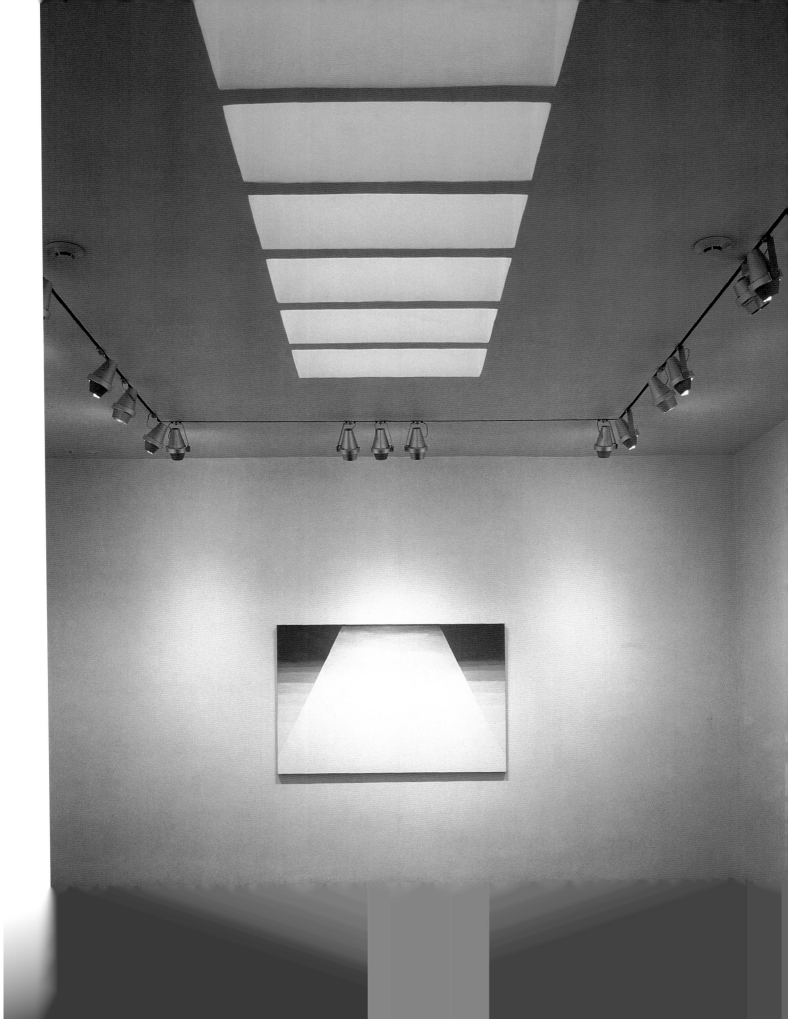

32 | DIA CENTER FOR THE ARTS 545 II 1997

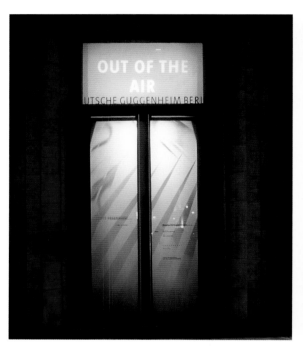

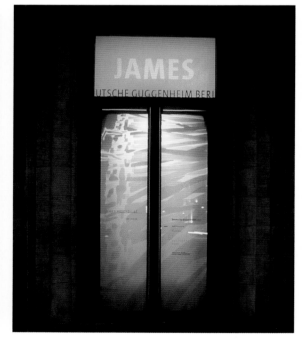

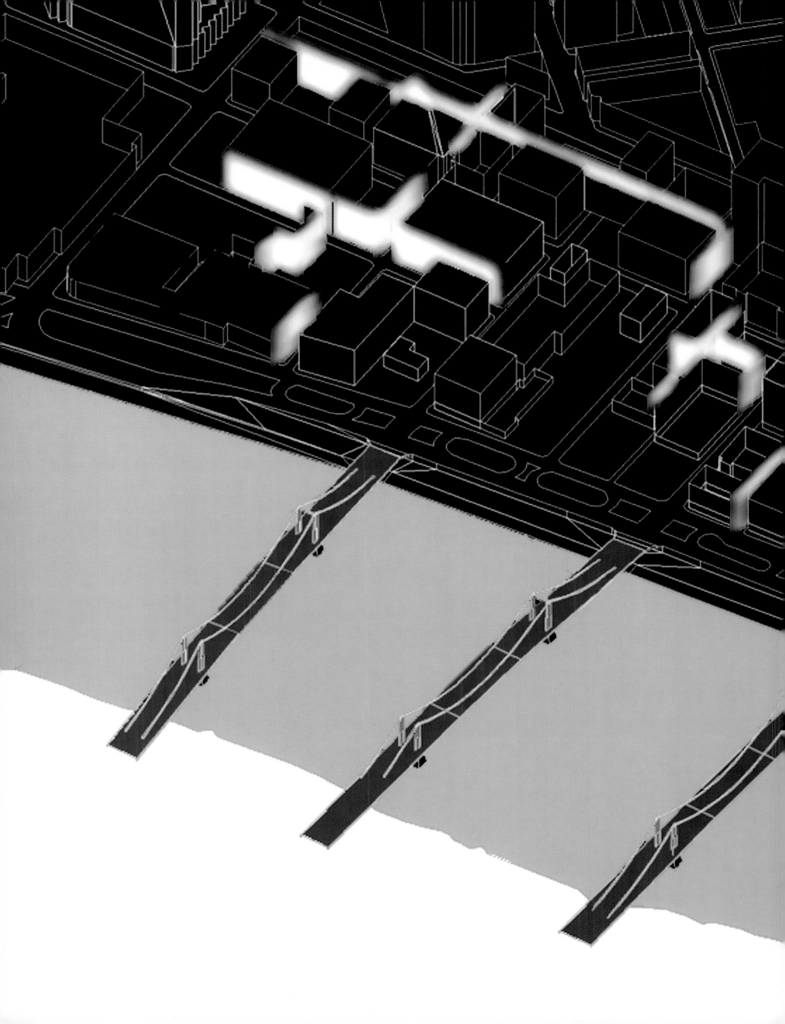

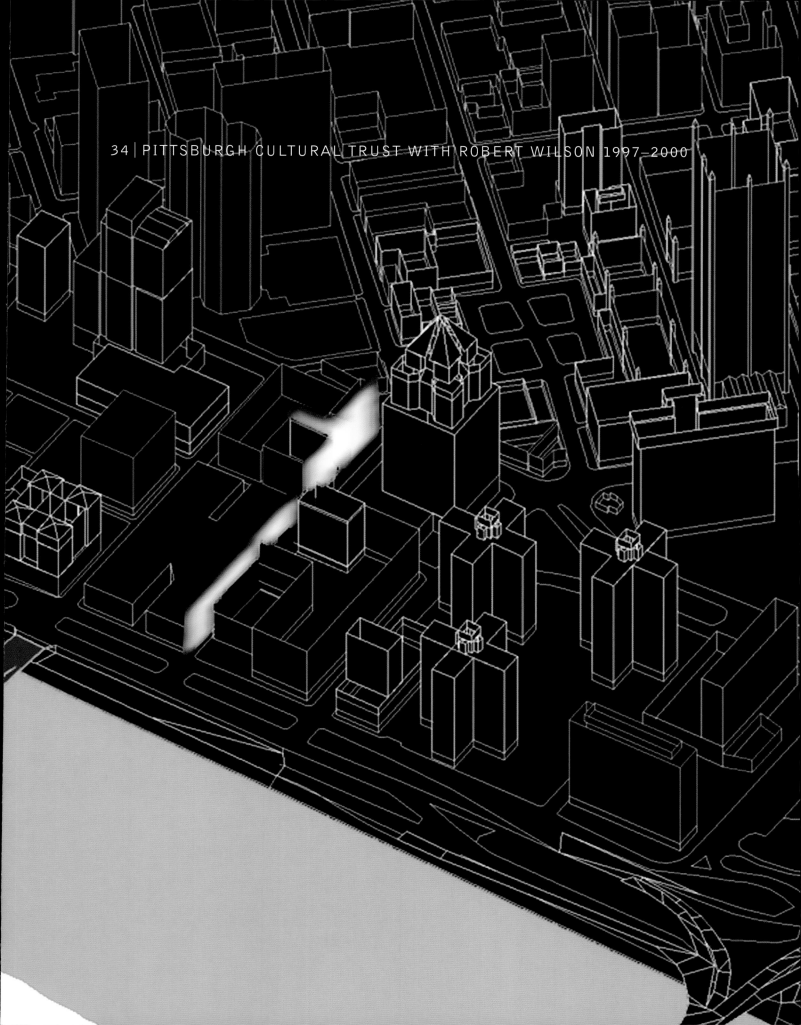

35│HELMUT LANG BOUTIQUE 1998

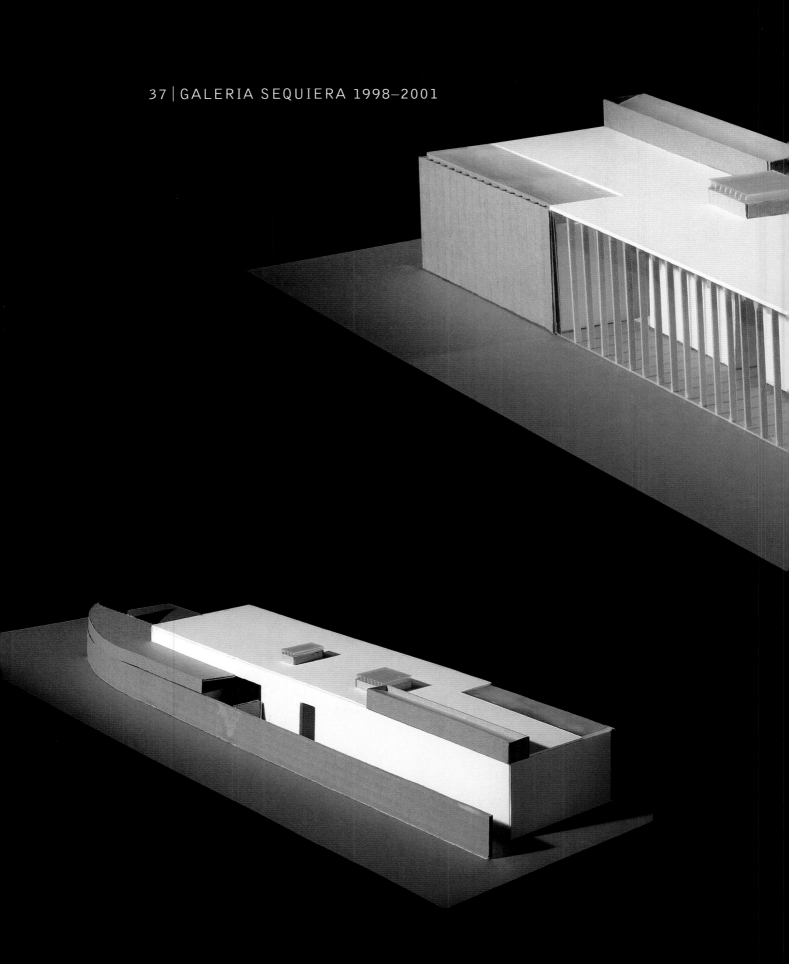

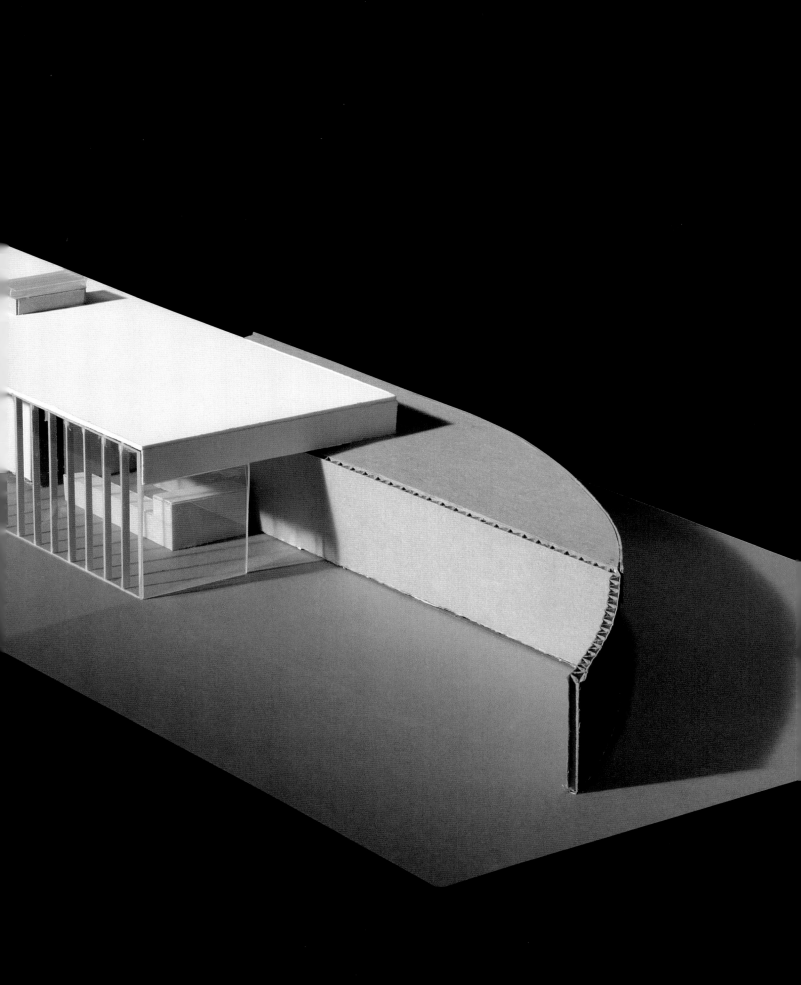

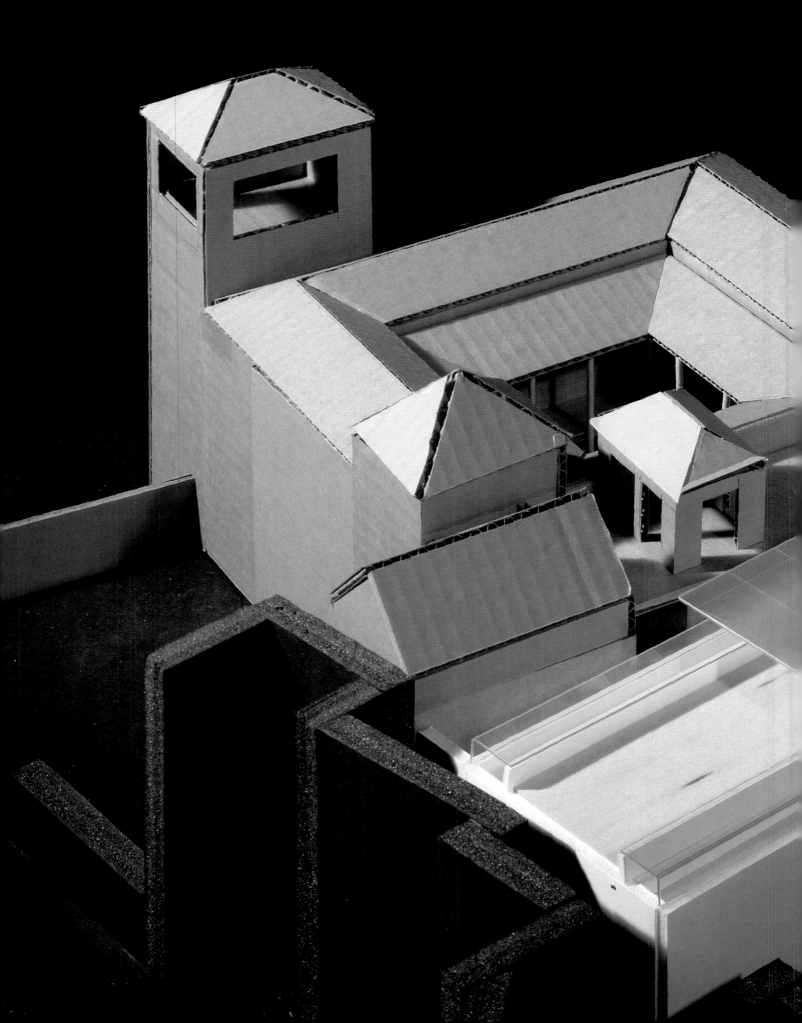

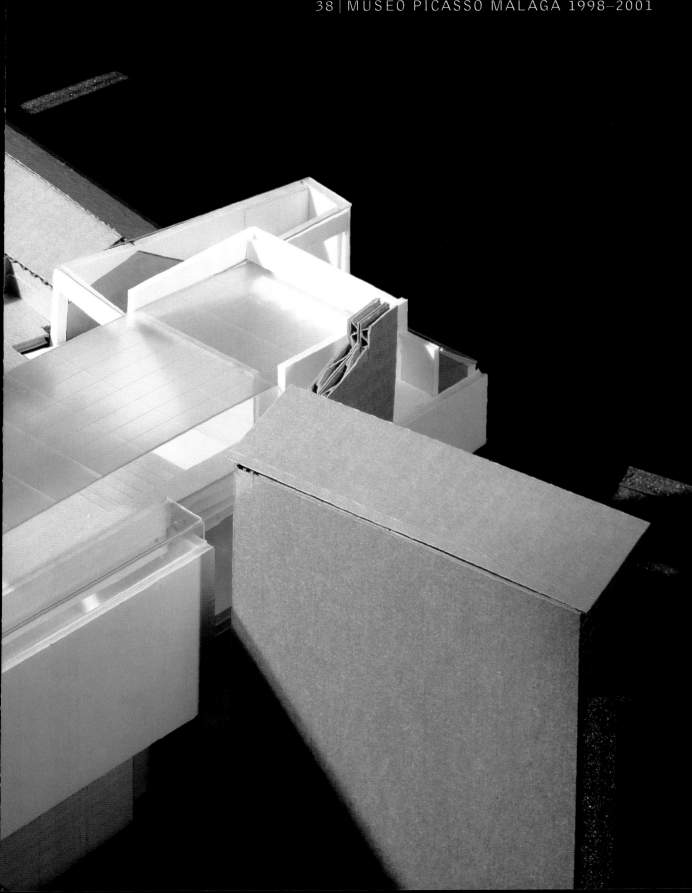

SPACE FRAMED

Richard Gluckman

For the past twenty years I have been working with artists, curators, and directors. Heiner Friedrich and Philippa de Menil, founders of the Dia Art Foundation in New York, introduced me to contemporary art by hiring me to work on the renovation of their town house on Manhattan's Upper East Side. Their private art collection included works by Cy Twombly, Blinky Palermo, Walter de Maria, Donald Judd, and Dan Flavin. These artists were invited to install their work in the house during the process of construction, giving me my first exposure to a new kind of art. Heiner Friedrich's specific directive was "Do not design." Paraphrasing Louis Kahn, he asked me to "open my eyes" and "let the spaces be what they want to be." Dan Flavin's fluorescent light installations were particularly significant to me. In one, his understanding of the existing architecture and the way in which he placed his lights to echo original architectural details both respected the earlier vernacular and animated the space with a newer technology. In another, he transformed the renovation of the main stair into a shaft of multicolored light that seemed to emanate from an existing glass laylight.

In the late 1970s I acted as a kind of "expeditor" to some of the same artists on a series of installations at 393 West Broadway. The installations included work by Fred Sandback, Cy Twombly, Donald Judd, John Chamberlain, the initial installation of **Shadows** by Andy Warhol, an extraordinary installation by Dan Flavin, and the installation of **The Broken Kilometer** by Walter de Maria. Later, I worked more closely with Dan Flavin on the proposed intervention to Dick's Castle, a 30,000-square-foot reinforced concrete structure in Garrison, New York, and the renovation to a Baptist church, originally a firehouse, in Bridgehampton, New York. Here again, Flavin carefully accentuated the existing architecture with his arrays of fluorescent light. Gradually I have been privileged to work with other artists such as Jenny Holzer, Robert Wilson, and Richard Serra on a variety of projects from their inception. This experience has informed me of the relationship between art and architecture. At times ambiguous, the line dissolved between the two, establishing a deliberate tension, an interactive relationship that is mutually critical.

My exposure to minimalist art complemented my earlier education at Syracuse University, where my teachers were young, talented second-generation modernists. They drilled into us the principles of Frank Lloyd Wright, Le Corbusier, and Mies van der Rohe. Working in the offices of William Scarbrough, Lou Skoler, Kermit Lee, and Werner Seligmann provided a strong professional structure in a positive design environment.

Certain journeys stand out as formative experiences as well. As a student, on a travel fellowship with my friend and, later, partner Frederick Stelle, I made a tour of Europe to see monuments of modern architecture in Holland and Scandinavia. Another trip across Italy with Tiffany Bell, an art critic who became my wife, made me aware of a deeper dimension to the site-specific art to which I was exposed in New York. This trip began in Milan, at the refectory containing Leonardo da Vinci's **Last Supper**, and continued to Varese to see Count Panza di Biumo's eighteenth-century villa and stables. These were installed with contemporary art, and we explored this series of chapel-like spaces, each transformed in a different way by each artist's work. We continued to Giotto's Scrovegni Chapel in Padua and arrived in Rome. There the Caravaggio paintings in the small chapel in Santa Maria del Popolo formed an ensemble that was a powerful precedent for some of the art installations that I was seeing in New York.

It seemed to me that the potential for substantial architecture lay in the sense of immediacy in time and place generated by the relationship between artwork and the space it inhabited. Certain contemporary artists used architectural means to establish a new and immediate relationship between the viewer, the object, and the space around it. The materiality of the work became significant. The artwork was given a more active presence, engaging and confronting the viewer in real space.

Like the minimalist artists, I try to create architecture in which the viewer is compelled to consider his place in real space and time. Less architectural detail and decor allows for more emphasis on the basic architectural components: structure, scale, proportion, material, and light. My approach is neither reductive nor neutral. The simple appearance allows the space to respond to what will go in it, rather than to recede or dissolve. In the design of art exhibition space it is imperative to create spaces that interact positively with the art to come. Therefore I seek to create a frame, both structural and volumetric, that becomes complete and unified by the art and, by extension, the viewer in a future from which the designer is excluded. I have found that this approach works equally well with residential and commercial architecture.

I am an intuitive designer. It is my immediate experience with builders, clients, curators, and artists that has most informed my work. This cumulative experience is leading me and the architects I work with into new territories. Recent projects in Braga, Portugal; Malaga, Spain; Raleigh, North Carolina; and Austin, Texas, are new opportunities to practice the language we have spent so long learning. It is the language of surface and materiality, lightness and weight, shadow and light, scale and proportion, frame and space.

Illuminated Structure,
Embodied Space
Hal Foster

1 Reyner Banham, **A Concrete Atlantis**: U.S. Industrial Building and European Modern Architecture (Cambridge, Mass.: MIT Press, 1986).

2 See Beatriz Colomina, **Privacy and Publicity: Modern Architecture as Mass Media** (Cambridge, Mass.: MIT Press, 1994).

3 In what follows I am indebted to Terence Riley, **Light Construction** (New York: Museum of Modern Art, 1995), and to Joanna Merwood, "Herzog and de Meuron and the Blurring of 'Transparency'," unpublished paper, School of Architecture, Princeton University, 1998.

CONCRETE ATLANTIS

The first capital of America for European architects like Walter Gropius and Le Corbusier was not New York or Chicago; it was Buffalo. Long before these architects ever visited this country, they sought a historical precedent for rationalist architecture without ornament, and they found it in such industrial structures as the grain elevators that line the riverfront of Buffalo, a transportation hub between the Midwest and the East. For the Europeans these structures were formed by function alone, or at least they could be made to appear so. (When Le Corbusier published two photographs of such buildings in **L'Esprit nouveau** and **Vers une architecture**, he removed details that distracted from this reading, which essentially conflated functionalism with abstraction.) To look to savage America for an architectural origin in this way was a kind of primitivism, but it was a kind of futurism too, for the Europeans also saw America as the land of industrial production and mass society, which they anticipated as the imminent condition of all modern architecture. This European America, then, was a mythical place, at once primitive and futuristic, a paradoxical space-time captured nicely in the phrase "Concrete Atlantis," as coined by Reyner Banham in his 1986 study of the importance of these industrial buildings for the European moderns.[1]

Richard Gluckman was born in Buffalo, the capital of this Concrete Atlantis, in 1947, and its grain elevators and factories were formative for him as well. Yet they were neither exotic nor futuristic as they were for the moderns: however impressive, they were part of his everyday cityscape, and to a child of the television age they appeared outmoded. Thus his relation to both industrial architecture and structural transparency could only be one of reclamation — an attitude that Gluckman shared with a group of artists, mostly minimalists like Dan Flavin and Richard Serra, who were also raised in industrial centers in decline: These artists would come to influence Gluckman as well.

Already in the industrial architecture singled out by the moderns there was a tension between the obvious mass of the building and the apparent transparency of the structure. This structural transparency was complicated by another kind of transparency, for these buildings were first known to most Europeans as images alone, through photographs: thus mediated, these masses were somewhat dematerialized in reception.[2] This tension — between the materiality of structured spaces and the dematerialization of disembodied images — has become exacerbated in our own time, and, along with other prominent architects of his generation like Rem Koolhaas, Bernard Tschumi, Steven Holl, and Jacques Herzog and Pierre de Meuron, Gluckman has had to address it in his architecture.

All of these architects use new materials and techniques in different ways, and as a group they have returned the old modernist issue of transparency to architectural debate.[3] Perhaps no term is more important to Western architecture in the twentieth century. By the late 1920s the great architectural historian Siegfried Giedion pronounced structural transparency to be the primary characteristic of modern architecture. For Giedion this transparency was predicated on technologies, like steel, glass, and ferroconcrete, that allowed a thorough analysis of architectural

4 Here, as Merwood suggests, Moholy anticipates the contemporary attempt to transform different representations of space into different constructions of space.

5 Colin Rowe and Robert Slutzky, "Transparency: Literal and Phenomenal," Perspecta 8 (1963), 46. Ironically, whereas Giedion had associated literal transparency with cubism, Rowe and Slutzky associated phenomenal transparency with it.

6 This is how Riley describes the 1992 building for the Goetz Collection in Munich by Herzog and de Meuron in Light Construction, p. 11.

7 1963 marks the emergence of pop as well, which has also affected Gluckman indirectly, not only as the architect of the Andy Warhol Museum, but also, I will argue below, because minimalism and pop are aesthetic complements that can only be understood in relation to one another. For this relation see my The Return of the Real (Cambridge, Mass.: MIT Press, 1996).

space — a project pursued in analogous ways in other arts (e.g., Giedion understood cubist painting as such an analysis of pictorial space). By the 1930s the Bauhaus artist Lazlo Moholy-Nagy expanded the meaning of structural transparency. In his view this transparency might allow architecture to integrate the different transparencies advanced by other mediums like photography and film. Less concerned with space than light, Moholy saw this integration as fundamental to the "new vision" of modernist culture.[4] Yet this technophilic utopia of art and architecture did not fare well after the war, and by the mid-1950s structural transparency was no longer an automatic value. In a classic text on the subject written in 1955–56 but not published until 1963, Colin Rowe and Robert Slutzky devalued structural transparency (or "literal transparency"), in which deep space is revealed by means of clear glass or actual openings, in favor of structural ambiguity (or "phenomenal transparency"), in which shallow space is implied by means of "cubist" surfaces that "interpenetrate without optical destruction of each other."[5]

To favor phenomenal transparency over literal transparency seems like a minor revaluation of terms, but it may mark the moment when attention to surface draws even with concern for space in architectural production, and when a reading of skin becomes as important as an understanding of structure in architectural reception. That is to say, it may mark the moment when postmodern architecture is prepared, at least discursively, in its two principal versions: first, architecture as a scenographic surface of symbols (as in pastiche postmodernism from Robert Venturi on),

and, later, architecture as an autonomous transformation of forms (as in deconstructivist postmodernism from Peter Eisenman on). Like some of his peers, Gluckman does not fit neatly into either line. In fact he resisted both options (I will suggest how later) in order to recover a version of literal transparency on the one hand, and to develop a version of phenomenal transparency (through surfaces that are often more luminous scrim than planar skin) on the other. In part this project is shared by peers like Koolhaas and Herzog and de Meuron, but Gluckman does not recover literal transparency and develop phenomenal transparency in order to undo them, as they often do; his is by no means "a complete reversal of the structural clarity of the so-called Miesian glass box."[6] In a sense this difference stems from a different point of origin, a different retrospect on "1963," as it were. For Gluckman 1963 marks less the advocacy of phenomenal transparency by Rowe and Slutzky than the emergence of minimalist art, whose architectural interventions have influenced him as much as the abstract masses of the Buffalo grain elevators influenced Gropius and Le Corbusier.[7]

DIAFIED BUILDING

In the late 1970s Gluckman, then a fledgling architect in New York, met the German art dealer Heiner Friedrich, who, with Philippa de Menil, had founded the Dia Art Foundation in 1974. The foundation supported the projects of several artists and composers of the minimalist generation — Dan Flavin, Donald Judd, Walter de Maria, Robert Whitman, and LaMonte Young among them — through the development of exhibition and performance spaces. Often involved with industrial materials, structures, and techniques, minimalist art was scaled to industrial space. Often made in such spaces (e.g., in old lofts), it was fitting to exhibit it there as well (e.g., in old warehouses). Indeed the emergence of minimalism coincided with the transformation of SoHo from a light-industrial neighborhood into an art community, and with the expansion of exhibition spaces beyond the old palace-model of the museum-gallery.

Aware of these developments, Friedrich retained Gluckman to scout appropriate buildings in Manhattan. An early project was the conversion of a SoHo loft building (ca. 1890) at 393 West Broadway, originally a mixed-use structure (retail below, manufacturing and storage above). Gluckman transformed it into an open space ordered by the original columns — a perfect foil for the serial objects and images of the Dia artists. (He associates this reductivist mantra with Friedrich: "Don't design. Strip the room to its essentials so you know what it's about.") Gluckman helped to install **The Broken Kilometer** by de Maria (which remains there), a floor piece of a thousand bronze rods one meter in length that not only articulates the space but measures it as well. This was art, Gluckman came to see of such minimalism, that framed architecture as it was framed by it, that posed a dialogical relation with structure and space from which he could learn. The next Dia projects focused on Flavin, including the conversion of a Bridgehampton firehouse into an installation space in the early 1980s. The fluorescent lights used by Flavin both articulate the given architecture and produce a luminous spatiality that exceeds it. In

so doing he may have encouraged Gluckman to expose structure and to suggest space at once, to develop literal and phenomenal transparencies in tandem, rather than to privilege the one over the other or indeed to oppose the two at all.

The next rite of passage occurred in the mid-1980s when Gluckman converted a mixed-use Chelsea loft building (ca. 1909) into exhibition spaces for the Dia Center. Although only two decades newer than the SoHo warehouse, this five-floor structure represents an advance in engineering over the earlier building. Its reinforced concrete supports a greater span than the wood joists of the SoHo type, and so its spaces are broader. This expanse suited the installation practices of the artists invited by Dia to work there, most of whom are legatees of minimalist, pop, and/or conceptual art. It also suited Gluckman, who opened up the warehouse in such a way as to allow its structure to clarify the exhibition spaces. This strategy of addition through subtraction allowed the exhibition spaces in turn to frame the artist projects. The spaces work both ways: they can frame the art when required (as in the beautiful Robert Ryman exhibition of 1988–89), or be framed by the art when it projects a space of its own (as in the luminous Robert Irwin installation of 1998).

Thus, even as the Dia Center was designed for such art, the architecture was informed by it, and this minimalist initiation allowed Gluckman to resist the blandishments of postmodernism (which were very strong in the mid-1980s) in its dominant modes of pastiche and deconstruction. Gluckman was more interested in the latter than the former; for example, he shares with deconstructivist postmodernism an indirect connection to Russian constructivism. Yet he comes to constructivist principles via minimalists like Flavin and Andre, who helped to recover the principles of Vladmir Tatlin and Alexander Rodchenko in the early 1960s. Flavin and Andre stressed the transparency of construction in constructivism — a principle also advanced by Serra, with whom Gluckman has worked closely. This constructivism is very different from the deconstructivist version, which is more concerned with disturbance of space than transparency of construction. So, too, this constructivist lineage has distanced Gluckman not only from the cubist preoccupations of the school of Rowe and Slutzky, but also from the media seductions of contemporary architecture that chases after the Information Zeitgeist.

A MUSEUM FOR WARHOL

In 1989 Gluckman began to design a solo museum for Andy Warhol in Pittsburgh, the hometown of the artist. This was another conversion of an industrial building (ca. 1911), originally occupied by the Frick and Lindsay Company, which supplied machine tools to the steel industry. Here, however, the project was a complete museum, with auditorium, movie theater, offices, study center, store, and café. It thus differed programatically from the **Kunsthalle** format of the Dia Center, just as the pop of Warhol differs structurally from the minimalist fare of the original Dia. Indeed Warhol represents the other side of the dialectic of American art in the 1960s, for if most minimalists evoked the repetitive objects of industrial production, Warhol evoked the serial images of mass consumption.

With this difference in mind, another architect might have proposed a postindustrial media center as the most appropriate program. Instead Gluckman wisely elaborated the structural clarity of the industrial building into a strong foil for the mediated imagery of Warhol. Thus, for the great **Elvis** silkscreens Gluckman bared the beams of the ceiling, and for the panoramic **Shadow** paintings he chamfered the columns of the room in such a way as to punctuate these long image sequences. In effect he used minimalist units like beams and columns to frame the pop images. An extraordinary effect of these sequences is not only to dematerialize the image but to disembody the viewer; sometimes these spectral series seem almost to drain you of your body. To register the uncanny dematerialization at work in the **Shadows**, say, or to feel the deathly disembodiment in the **Skulls** (which operates on the thematic level too), requires the foil of an embodied space; that is, it requires that the viewer be framed as well. And Gluckman delivers this structured embodiment effectively, sometimes with the materiality of beams and columns, sometimes with the luminosity of scrims and skylights, and other devices of scale and light.

It is this sympathetic structuring that makes the Warhol Museum a model for museums of contemporary art. Unfortunately it is not much followed: the prevalent tendencies in museum architecture (where the example of Frank Lloyd Wright at the Guggenheim Museum rules over the example of Louis Kahn at the Kimball Museum) are to trump the art — either to use the mediated aspect of the pop trajectory of art as a pretext for a semidissolved architecture-as-cinema (as

8 This dialectic is somewhat different in prewar art. There it is often acted out between idealist form and materialist articulation of substance and site, as is evident, for example, in the sculpture of Constantin Brancusi. A sense of this dialectic has made Gluckman an effective designer of exhibitions of such art—in particular the 1996 Brancusi show at the Philadelphia Museum of Art.

9 This may seem conservative to an architectural vanguard, but in a period when such spaces are either abandoned by the government or penetrated by the corporations, such acts of preservation can become progressive.

in some projects by Tschumi), or to use the great scale of the minimalist trajectory of art as a pretext for a grandiose architecture-as-spectacle (the "Bilbao Effect" of Frank Gehry). Neither option understands the art (in the literal sense of support): it competes with it, sometimes vanquishes it. And it tends to overwhelm the viewer as well: an "architectural sublime" shatters out aesthetic contemplation and critical reflection alike.

Gluckman proceeds otherwise in large part because he has learned from postwar art. In particular he has intuited the minimalist-pop dialectic, the tense relation between impulses to materialize and to dematerialize the object (architecture and art), to embody and to disembody the subject (the viewer).[8] This contradiction — between bodily reality and transcendental fantasy — is very strong in contemporary culture, and part of the appeal of Gluckman's architecture is that Gluckman addresses this contradiction indirectly, mediates it spatially. When appropriate, he privileges one impulse (to embody or to disembody), favors one transparency (literal or phenomenal), over the other. For example, for galleries focused on the minimalist trajectory of art (like the Paula Cooper or the Larry Gagosian galleries), Gluckman has designed structured spaces that echo the constructive concerns and bodily effects of this art. On the other hand, for homes and small museums, he has produced luminous spaces often by means of scrims and skylights. In homes (like the Wright or the Krauss-Hollier residences) this illumination can create a place of calm interiority (it can also suggest more space than in fact exists). In small museums (like the Georgia O'Keeffe Museum in

Santa Fe) it can create a place of quiet reflection well suited to the art.[9]

Yet this play with phenomenal transparency can also dazzle or simply confuse. What elicits contemplation in a private setting can produce mystification in a public setting. Such architecture can become an illuminated sculpture, a radiant jewel, as is sometimes the case with Herzog and de Meuron. The effect is often beautiful, enigmatic — and spectacular in the negative sense of Guy Debord, the great critic of consumer capitalism. That is, such architecture can become a kind of commodity-fetish on a grand scale, a mysterious object whose structure and construction cannot be decoded. Gluckman is not free of this fetishistic design, this cold seduction, in his work for fashion clients (e.g., the Helmut Lang boutique in SoHo, the Gianni Versace project in Miami), for whom, perhaps, it is only too appropriate.

AN INCOMPLETE PROJECT
Gluckman was not much affected by the dominant versions of postmodern architecture —scenographic surface or deconstructed form. He also poses an alternative to the two current positions that complicate the two postmodern ones. For both these current positions literal transparency is tied to industrial structure, and so can only be outmoded in our postindustrial present: it can only mystify new media and technologies that cannot be made evident, let alone reflexive, in the old modernist ways. What is structural integrity or tectonic clarity, when, with advanced materials and techniques, almost anything can be designed, engineered, and built? The first position,

10 Herzog quoted in Riley, **Light Construction**, p. 20. This position is thus not too far from scenographic postmodernism, even if it does not indulge in pop-historical allusions. Indeed such architecture adds modernism as another image, another surface for projection, to the postmodern pastiche-repertoire.

11 Riley, **Light Construction**, p. 16. Riley means this description appreciatively, and he alludes to **The Large Glass** (1915–23) of Marcel Duchamp as a model of "light construction" that creates enigmatic surfaces and ambiguous spaces. But such architecture can be seen as a kind of cold seduction, as a kind of "bachelor machine."

12 Anthony Vidler, **The Architectural Uncanny** (Cambridge, Mass.: MIT Press, 1992), p. 221. Vidler refers here to Koolhaas, but I find this description more appropriate to Herzog and de Meuron.

13 I develop here on an unpublished note on Richard Gluckman by Rosalind Krauss in which she applies the Habermasian notion of modernity as "an incomplete project" to his architecture. See Jürgen Habermas, "Modernity—An Incomplete Project," in Hal Foster, ed., **The Anti-Aesthetic** (Seattle: Bay Press, 1983).

14 Krauss, ibid.

represented by Herzog and de Meuron, concludes that an architecture of surface — "surfaces for projection" — should be privileged over an architecture of space.[10] The second position, represented by Koolhaas or Tschumi, continues to focus on space, but it tends to dissolve it beyond any deconstruction — to montage it according to a quasi-cinematic model of broken flows.

Gluckman offers an alternative to both positions; his is neither a conflation of architecture and representation, as often in Herzog and de Meuron, nor a conversion of architecture into narrative or event, as often in Koolhaas or Tschumi. At stake here are philosophical implications for subjectivity and society, not just stylistic differences in design. If modern architecture valued literal transparency, it presupposed rationalist subjectivity in doing so: subjects were invited to understand space, to critique architecture, to defetishize culture. For us today this subject is in part a myth of its own to demystify. But what are the alternatives advanced in contemporary architecture? Pastiche postmodernism models a subject who seems to be master of architectural history, able to cite it at will, but in fact this subject is bombarded by amnesiac allusions. Conversely, deconstructivist postmodernism models a subject who seems at the mercy of architectural language, but in fact this subject is willful in its formal manipulations. The subjects interpellated by Herzog and de Meuron and Koolhaas or Tschumi are different again. The first tends to be seduced by the ambiguity of surface but removed from "the continuum of space."[11] Conversely, the second is plunged into "the continuum of space" but only to be almost dissolved there. Both subjects

are mystified by such architectures, "suspended in a difficult moment between knowledge and blockage" in the first instance, delivered over to a semideranged space in the second.[12]

The subject suggested by Gluckman is different still — neither rationalist as in most modern architecture (his spaces embody the subject too much for this to be the case), nor irrationalist as in most postmodern architecture. It may be that modernist transparency now mystifies more than it demystifies — that it cannot reveal the technological basis of contemporary building or anything else in contemporary society. But is this pretext enough to produce an architecture of obfuscation, one that tends to reinforce a subjectivity and society given over to commodity-fetishism, coded information, schizo spectacle? Rather than cancel modern architecture or simply cite it, architects might develop its "incomplete project" in other ways.[13] They might use advanced materials, techniques, and structures, but in order to register "new phenomenologies of bodily experience" rather than to promise a cyberspace beyond such experience, in order to invite "critical reflection" rather than to promise ecstatic illusion.[14] Richard Gluckman points one way to such an architecture.

PROJECT DESCRIPTIONS

   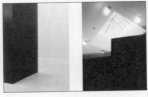

2 | FRIEDRICH GALLERY   4 | MARY BOONE GALLERY   6 | GAGOSIAN GALLERY   8 | HELMUT LANG BOUTIQUE
                        5 | HOUSE FOR AN   9 | GAGOSIAN GALLERY
                            ARTIST AND A WRITER

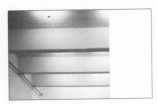

10 | DIA CENTER FOR THE
     ARTS 548

01|GLUCKMAN RESIDENCE, GLENWOOD, NEW YORK, 1968

14|15   16|17

Light and privacy were primary considerations in developing the design for this 2,100-square-foot house on a steep ravine in the hills south of Buffalo, encircled by tall pine trees and accessible to ski trails. A 9-by-24-foot skylight, facing south, lights both the central and upper levels. The lower level is open to the ravine. A circular retaining wall encloses a light well and diverts water around the building.

The two major, interlocking geometric forms of the house are identical in plan and section and foster a sense of internal intimacy without sacrificing the house's relationship to the external environment. They also create a distinctive architectural silhouette and prevent the buildup of snow and ice on the roofs.

02 | DIVIS RESIDENCE, FIRE ISLAND, NEW YORK, 1969

18|19

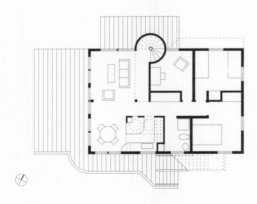

In the reconstruction and addition to a 25-by-34-foot box, the designer explored the notions of privacy, enclosure, and exposure on this site on Fire Island by exploiting man-made and natural elements to create different types of external space. The external form of the cylindrical stair enclosure, integrated into the basic rectilinear form of the house, has become a landmark for area fishermen. Sections of each deck can be "folded up" to serve as storm shutters to protect the sliding glass doors.

03 | FRIEDRICH/DE MENIL RESIDENCE, NEW YORK, NEW YORK, 1977

20 | 21

This renovation of a five-story town house for Heiner Friedrich and Philippa de Menil, the founders of the Dia Art Foundation, involved the integration of site-specific works by artist Dan Flavin and included the installation of work by Walter de Maria, Blinky Palermo, Cy Twombly, and Donald Judd.

04|INSTALLATION FOR **THE NEW YORK EARTH ROOM**, NEW YORK, NEW YORK, 1979
05|INSTALLATION FOR **THE BROKEN KILOMETER**, NEW YORK, NEW YORK, 1980
 BY WALTER DE MARIA

22|23   24|25

The renovation of the space housing **The New York
Earthroom** was our first exposure to the site-specific work
of Walter de Maria. Subsequently we worked with the
artist on the installation of **The Broken Kilometer**, the last
in a series of artists' installations at 393 West Broadway.

06 | FARRAGUT SHELTER, SAINT-GAUDENS NATIONAL HISTORIC SITE, CORNISH, NEW HAMPSHIRE, 1983

26|27   28|29

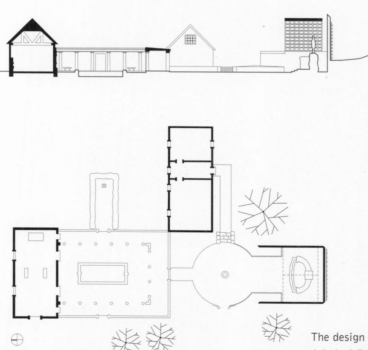

The design of a shelter for the original base of the Admiral Farragut Monument at the Saint-Gaudens National Historic Site. The structure's simple vocabulary of stucco, reinforced concrete, painted wood, and lead-coated copper was intended to reinforce the shelter's relationship with the existing complex of buildings and provide three basic functions: retaining wall, backdrop, and shelter.

07 | DIA CENTER FOR THE ARTS,
548 WEST TWENTY-SECOND STREET, NEW YORK , NEW YORK, 1987

30|31   32|33   34|35   36|37

38|39   40|41   42|43

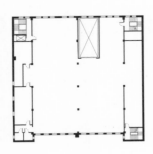  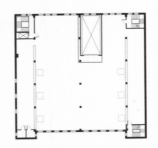

The renovation and conversion of a Chelsea Warehouse into a 40,000-square-foot exhibition facility at 548 West Twenty-second Street has become a model for exhibition facilities of this type. Since opening in 1987, the building has undergone additional renovation. The design's rigorous approach to space and detail emphasizes the sympathetic presentation of contemporary art.

08 | THE ANDY WARHOL MUSEUM, PITTSBURGH, PENNSYLVANIA, 1994

44|45

46|47

48|49

50|51

52|53

54|55

56|57

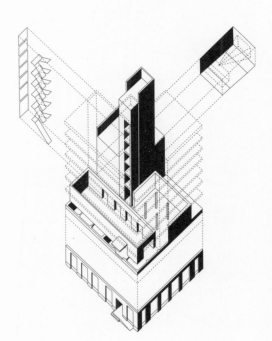

This eight-level, 85,000-square-foot renovation is the
largest single artist museum in the United States.
Exhibition space comprises approximately 35,000 square
feet of the building, with 10,000 square feet for archives
and collection storage. The balance of the building contains
an archival study center, administrative offices, an education department, a store, a café, and a 110-seat theater.

The renovation to this brick and terra-cotta building of
1911–17 employs a clear strategy toward orientation and
circulation to enhance the museological experience. The
experience is modulated by different architectural events,
in particular the removal of floor structure and one column
to create a cubed space at the metaphoric heart of the
building. At the entry, the walls, floor, ceiling, and doors
converge on the self-portrait on the opposite wall. The cross
of the entry doors is superimposed over this portrait.

09 | RYMAN PAVILION, PHARMAKON '90, TOKYO, JAPAN, 1990

58 | 59

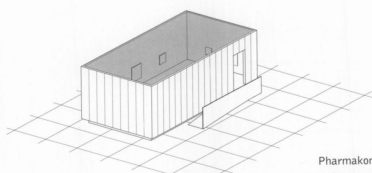

Pharmakon '90 was an exhibit of seventy-one international artists, organized for the purpose of bringing contemporary international art to Tokyo, Japan. This office worked with the painter Robert Ryman to build a pavilion for the presentation of his work. The 18-by-36-foot room was slightly elevated above the convention hall floor and covered with a fabric scrim to filter the ambient light in the hall.

10|WRIGHT LOFT, NEW YORK, NEW YORK, 1990

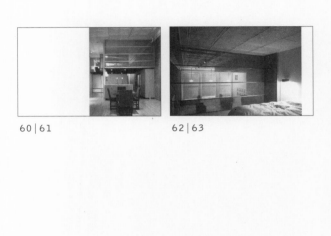

60|61   62|63

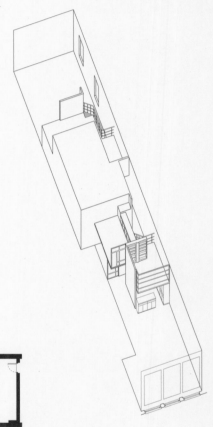

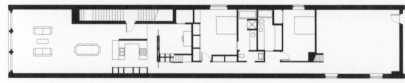

This intervention into a residential loft for an artist and his family included the addition of children's rooms, a guest room, a private study, and a television room. A series of mezzanines was introduced around the existing core, using steel and glass doors, and stainless steel mesh to create varying degrees of transparent, translucent, and opaque enclosure.

11 | GORDON RESIDENCE, NEW YORK, NEW YORK, 1990

64 | 65   66 | 67

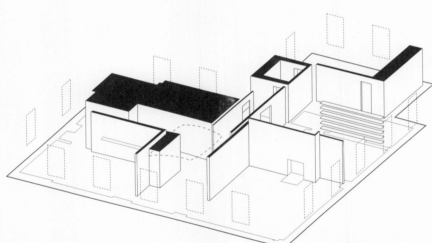

This apartment in the San Remo building occupies an
entire floor of one of the building's two distinctive towers.
To emphasize this privileged location, the perimeter of
the apartment was cleared of all partitions. The existing
exterior walls are covered with a tinted wall treatment
matching the exterior brick and marked by a continuous
stone border. Main living spaces are defined by nested
L-shaped walls, which do not touch the perimeter walls.
The interior core is clad with stone referring to the materials in the building's lobby. In this apartment the architect also explores the ways in which artificial light is
introduced into a space, altering the qualities of the space
as daylight fades and the views of Central Park disappear.

12 | ROW RESIDENCE, CUSHING ISLAND, MAINE, 1991–1996

68 | 69   70 | 71   72 | 73

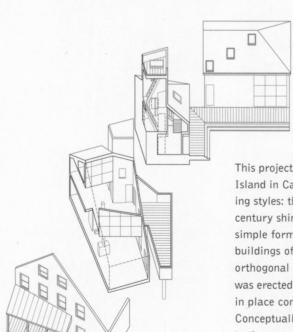

This project for an artist and graphic designer is on Cushing Island in Casco Bay. The island has had three distinct building styles: the first includes many cottages in the nineteenth-century shingle style by John Calvin Stevens; second, the simple forms and colors of the brick, granite, and slate buildings of the World War I army base, laid out in a rigid orthogonal grid adjacent to the site; the third building type was erected prior to Word War II and consisted of poured in place concrete observation towers and fortifications. Conceptually, the house responds in an arbitrary manner to the vernacular of all three. Each distinct volume contains a different function: living spaces, stair and bedroom tower, painting studio, and sun porch. Each volume uses a shape and color that recalls the earlier constructed forms on the island. The volumes are then assembled into a whole and are sited to frame particular views and identify navigational lines of position at the entrance to Portland harbor.

13 | GAGOSIAN GALLERY, NEW YORK, NEW YORK, 1991

74 | 75   76 | 77

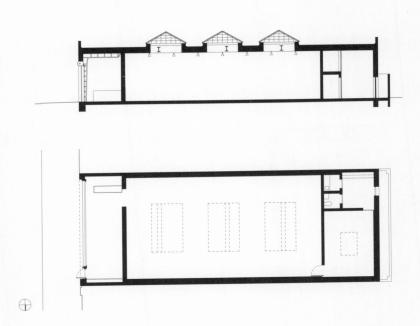

The Gagosian Gallery in SoHo is a large one-room exhibition space for contemporary art. All that remains of the former Wooster Street garage is the brick facade. The floor, walls, and roof structure were replaced to maximize ceiling height and increase the floor's loading capacity. The simple vernacular of plastic skylights, steel beams, concrete, and aluminum and glass garage door is a response to an earlier industrial vocabulary. The relationship of beams to skylight openings was deliberately skewed to animate the ceiling plane.

14 | DIA CENTER FOR THE ARTS,
545 WEST TWENTY-SECOND STREET, NEW YORK, 1992

78 | 79

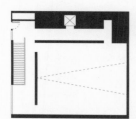 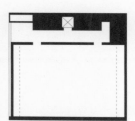 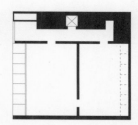 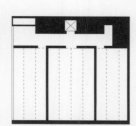

This 40,000-square-foot, four-story exhibition facility for the Dia Center for the Arts was conceived primarily for extended installations from Dia's own collection. The building's construction responds to the surrounding warehouse vernacular using steel, masonry block, and glass; the building is a contemporary interpretation of early-twentieth-century American industrial architecture. The facade of the new building is sheathed almost entirely with glass of varying levels of transparency. Curators, by manipulating a simple system of interior walls, which constitute a second facade, are able to regulate the amount of daylight entering the galleries. The dense core contains the ancillary functions and supports the open exhibition spaces.

15 | DIA CENTER FOR THE ARTS,
535 WEST TWENTY-SECOND STREET, NEW YORK, 1992

80 | 81

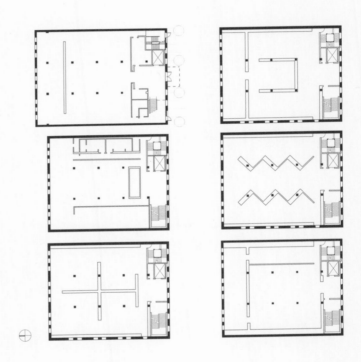

The design of the renovation to 535 shifted the elevator and stair core to the first bay of the building. This relatively dense structural grid was carefully interpreted into designs for specific artists' work from the permanent collection. Beams, slabs, and columns were partially removed at the top floor to relieve the pervasive structure and frame the sky-lights. The building program also accomodates a flat-floored auditorium for dance performances, symposia, and lectures.

16 | THE ANDY WARHOL FOUNDATION FOR THE VISUAL ARTS, NEW YORK, NEW YORK, 1993

82 | 83

84 | 85

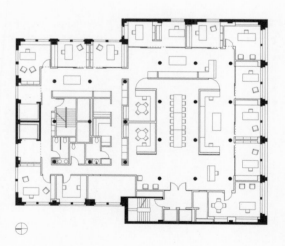

The renovation of a 7,500-square-foot floor for the foundation offices is in Louis Sullivan's landmarked Bayard Building. The offices are defined by an enclosing translucent wall composed of fixed panels and sliding doors, taking advantage of the building's large windows and allowing a maximum of natural light. The central space may be fully enclosed for meetings or opened as a gallery.

17 | SOUTH CENTRAL FIRST CITY, WITH FOX & FOWLE, WUHAN, PEOPLES REPUBLIC OF CHINA, 1993

86 | 87   88 | 89

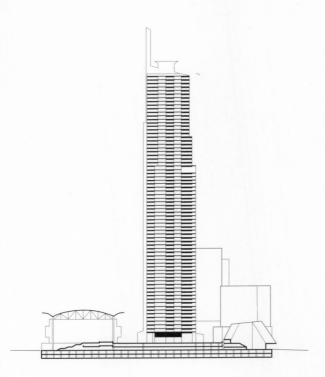

This invited competition for a new urban development includes a seventy-story office tower, an exhibition hall, a hotel, a financial building, a retail complex, and residential apartments. This project was one of several that are the result of the joint venture of Fox & Fowle, Gluckman, Liu.

18 | INSTALLATION FOR **LUSTMORD** BY JENNY HOLZER,
BARBARA GLADSTONE GALLERY, NEW YORK, NEW YORK, 1994

90 | 91

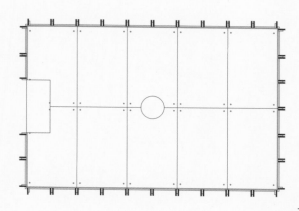

The architect worked with the artist to design and detail
this structure of wood, plywood, and leather.

19 | HOUSE FOR AN ARTIST AND A WRITER,
CAPE BRETON, NOVA SCOTIA, 1994

92 | 93   94 | 95   96 | 97

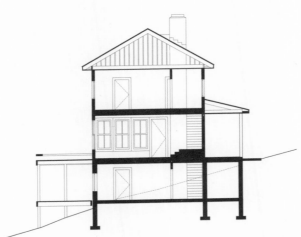

The house refers to the local vernacular archetype: a simple,
hip-roofed rectangular volume with an enclosed porch along
one long facade. Indigenous stone forms the lower level,
flanking storage room walls as well as the massive chimney,
which rises through all three floors. The chimney anchors
the house—an introspective counterpoint to the panoramic
ocean views visible from the living spaces. Interior walls and
ceilings are finished in painted tongue-and-groove boards,
the patterns of which relieve the white austerity. The detailing emphasizes the planar surface rather than demarcating
corner lines. Dark, solid floors, of either wenge wood or
Newfoundland slate, substantiate the floor planes with the
chimney mass.

20 | BERLIN HOLOCAUST MEMORIAL COMPETITION, WITH RICHARD SERRA, BERLIN, GERMANY, 1994

98|99

100|101

This project resulted from an invitation by the artist to collaborate on this competition located near the Brandenburg Gate. The ramp penetrates the ground plane to enter the elliptical form housing two stairs that descend 30 meters (to sea level) and a rectangular chamber open to the sky. Extruded through the form, the poché contains ancillary functions to support the program.

21 | WHITNEY MUSEUM OF AMERICAN ART, NEW YORK, NEW YORK, 1995–1998

102|103   104|105   106|107

This two-phase project was conceived to increase exhibition space within Marcel Breuer's 1966 architectural landmark and to consolidate the greatly dispersed staff of the institution. Phase one renovated two adjacent town houses and staff offices and included a tower that linked the three levels. Phase two transformed the museum's original office and library floors into exhibition space to house the Whitney's permanent collection and included restoration work throughout the museum. This plan supports Breuer's inverted structure by placing the foundation of the museum's collection at the top of the building.

22 | LEE LIES RESIDENCE, TESQUE, NEW MEXICO, 1995

108 | 109

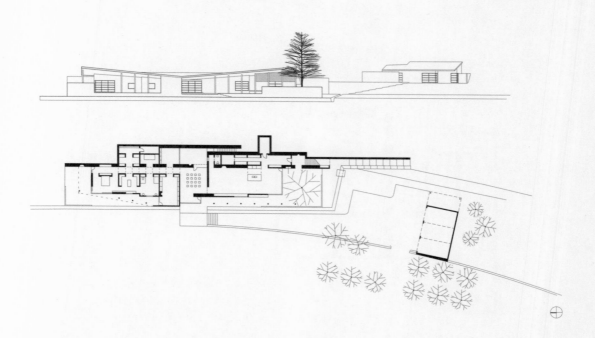

In this house for two art collectors in Tesque, New Mexico, the central space is designed around sixteen cast resin blocks by the English artist Rachel Whiteread. The house spirals off this central space into the private sector to the north and the public sector to the south. The house itself sits in a fracture of the land created by two ascequias (irrigation ditches that were once the lifeblood of the valley). The partially submerged service spaces anchor the house in the mesa rising to the east.

23 | MATCHBOX HOUSE, ORIENT, NEW YORK, 1995–1999

110|111

112|113

This weekend house for an urban family maximizes the surrounding wetland environment's relative calm. The home's elevated living spaces frame particular views, bedrooms and bathrooms are stacked, and interiors open onto porches and decks that cool the house. The master suite on the upper floor extends into an enclosed outdoor space that emphasizes the relationship with the sky and horizon.

24 | MARY BOONE GALLERY,
NEW YORK, NEW YORK, 1996

114 | 115

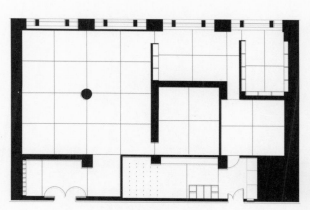

Mary Boone's Midtown gallery is a departure from the ubiqui-
tous white-walled gallery spaces. All surfaces are a tinted light
gray concrete and plaster with similar finishes, producing an
effect that blurs the distinction between floor, wall, and ceiling
planes. The enlarged central column suggests a strong vertical
axis in a predominantly horizontal space.

25 | PAULA COOPER GALLERY,
   NEW YORK, NEW YORK, 1996

116 | 117   118 | 119   120 | 121   122 | 123

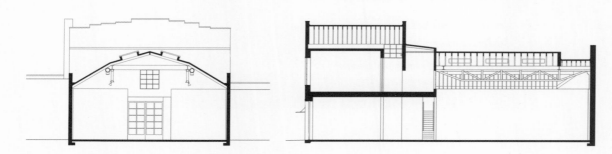

Reconstruction of a 6,500-square-foot warehouse. The floor structure was added to the nineteenth-century front building, which houses the entry, small gallery, and receiving with showroom, library, and offices upstairs. An intermediate structure was added to house stairs and elevator. Two pairs of trusses replace two columns in the main gallery. The interiors and details were chosen to sympathize with the heavy timber construction of the original structures.

26|THE MORI ART CENTER, TOKYO, JAPAN, 1996–2002

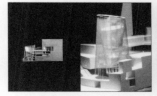

124|125   126|127

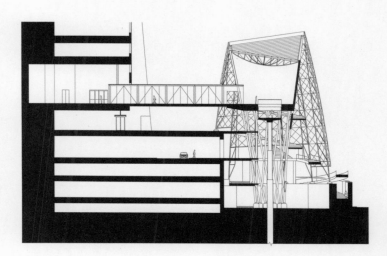

This 100,000-square-foot museum occupies the upper floors of a fifty-four-story office tower in Roppongi, Tokyo, designed by Kohn Pedersen Fox. The museum contains 30,000 square feet of exhibition space, a panoramic observation gallery, administrative offices, art handling spaces, education department, stores, and restaurants. Also included in the program is an entry pavilion at the base of the structure, linking parking, retail zones, and a plaza to the bridge entry at the lower museum lobby. This structure makes the cultural component of the tower and is sheathed in glass shingles on bow trusses tensioned to a concrete core.

27 | GIANNI VERSACE BOUTIQUE, NEW YORK, NEW YORK, 1998

128|129

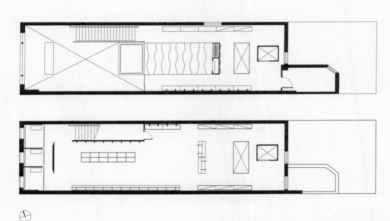

This transformation of a 7,500-square-foot, five-story town house on Madison Avenue replaces and repositions the floor structure to provide a two-story piano nobile at the front window. The main stair and elevator have been moved to the back of the building, creating a strong vertical axis that visually supports the horizontal planes. Interlocking voids form connections and allow natural light into the store. The perception of the surfaces is as much a visual as it is a tactile experience. Materials are deliberately chosen and emphasized where their intersection with the human body is encouraged or discouraged.

28 | VERSACE SOUTH BEACH, MIAMI, FLORIDA, 1997

130|131

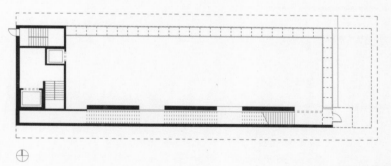

The architect conceived of a plan for a 19,200-square-foot, four-story structure using light as a major design element. The facade is a multidimensional grid of glass functioning dually as an enormous show window and a mutable reflector of changing light patterns using nematic liquid—crystal electrode film. It is able to be opaque, transparent, or translucent and works as a display window seen from both the inside and outside of the building. The interior plan is organized around a cascading stair on the south side of the structure. An overhanging canopy serves to shade the facade and reflect nighttime light.

29|MODERN ART MUSEUM, FORT WORTH, TEXAS, 1997

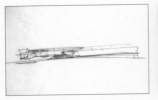

132|133

134|135

136|137

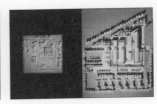

138|139

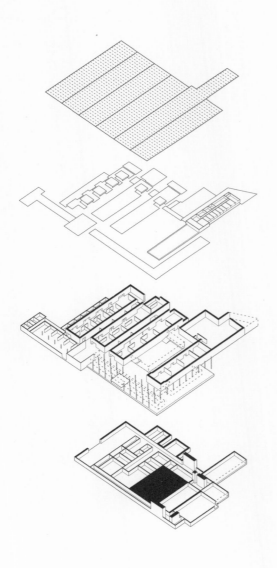

This 150,000-square-foot competition entry recognizes the evolution of the museum in careful consideration of architectural elements: proportion, scale, light, and materiality. The suites offer diversity of viewing areas with flexibility to accommodate a wide variety of art experiences. The naves create a contiguous narrative that can be joined from a number of entries. The entire structure is shielded by an expansive, translucent screen that floats overhead. Taking its position among the monuments of the district, the museum creates a place for contemplation and celebration.

30|ARTIST'S STUDIO, ACADIA SUMMER ARTS PROGRAM, MOUNT DESERT, MAINE, 1997

140|141   142|143   144|145

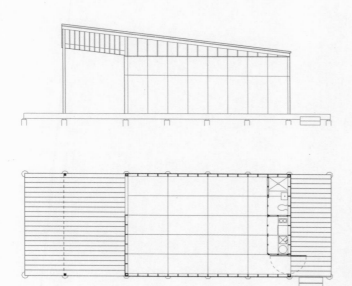

The Artist's Studio is a 1,200-square-foot building on a rural site in Maine. The external cladding consists of inexpensive industrial materials: cement board, polycarbonate glazing, and galvanized metal roofing. The interior suggests a higher level of local craftsmanship with carefully detailed wood framing and birch plywood paneling on the interior surfaces, with the exception of an L-shaped painting wall laminated with gypsum board. A small kitchen and bathroom are masked by sliding wood panels.

31 | GEORGIA O'KEEFFE MUSEUM, SANTA FE, NEW MEXICO, 1997

146 | 147   148 | 149

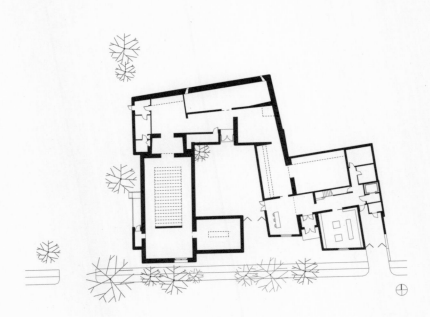

Located a short distance from the historic plaza in downtown Santa Fe, the museum is dedicated solely to the work
of Georgia O'Keeffe. The project involves the renovation of
and addition to an existing building providing 13,000 square
feet of space. By utilizing materials that refer to traditional
regional architecture and selectively introducing natural
light to the gallery spaces, it is the intent of the project to
provide an environment that subtly reinforces and enriches
the experience of viewing Georgia O'Keeffe's art.

32 | DIA CENTER FOR THE ARTS 545 II, NEW YORK, NEW YORK, 1997

150 | 151   152 | 153

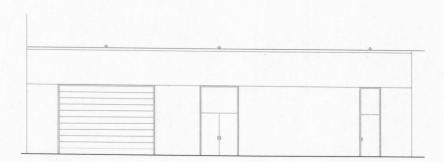

The renovation of this single-story bow-trussed building was intended for large-scale exhibitions. The early industrial vernacular was emphasized by the addition of painted brick walls. The facade was reworked to allow for the passage of both people and art into the building.

33|DEUTSCHE GUGGENHEIM BERLIN,
   BERLIN, GERMANY, 1997

154|155

156|157

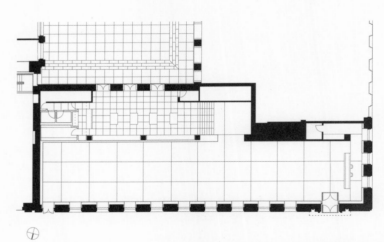

The Deutsche Guggenheim Berlin occupies the ground floor of the Berlin headquarters of the Deutsche Bank. In keeping with the elegant simplicity of the building, the museum consisits of a single exhibition hall and an elevated retail space, which opens onto the building's enclosed courtyard. Simple detailing, careful spatial proportioning, and a restrained palette of materials combine to create an environment of respectful sensitivity for the presentation of art.

34 | PITTSBURGH CULTURAL TRUST WITH ROBERT WILSON, PITTSBURGH, PENNSYLVANIA, 1997–2000

158 | 159   160 | 161

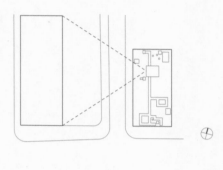

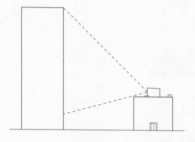

The office is currently working on the design of an "aesthetic enhancement" program for a major sixteen-block section of historic downtown Pittsburgh. Working in collaboration with Robert Wilson, the office was initially involved in a two-week workshop at the Watermill Center to focus on giving direction and shape to "distinctive and lively environments." Currently, Gluckman and Wilson are designing a number of light installations that exploit the edges and seams of the district: the rooftops, billboards, and service alleys.

35 | HELMUT LANG BOUTIQUE, NEW YORK, NEW YORK, 1998

162 | 163   164 | 165

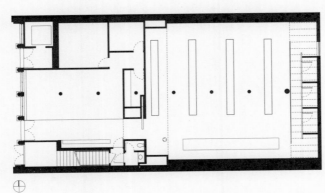

In this design of a 3,500-square-foot loft space in SoHo, the merchandising area has been placed toward the rear of the store, making the front space an ambiguous area visible from the street. A full translucent glass wall draws the customer to the rear space, where monolithic boxes in rigorous succession reveal themselves as freestanding cabinets containing the designer's collection. Behind the glass wall, a continuous skylight provides natural daylight to the dressing rooms. The Jenny Holzer installation provides an animated critical element in the quiet environment.

36 | SECOND STAGE WITH REM KOOLHAAS, NEW YORK, NEW YORK, 1999

166 | 167   168 | 169   170 | 171

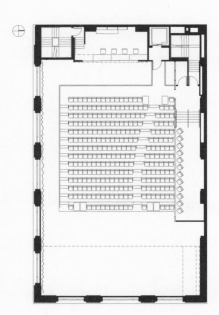

This is the second project this office has undertaken at the invitation of Rem Koolhaas. This collaborative effort is the renovation of a bank building into a 20,000-square-foot, 299-seat performing arts theater with rehearsal space, dressing rooms, offices, and public lobby. The architects sought to exploit the unique condition of the windowed wall with a moving curtain that emphasizes the transformative experience of the theater. The seating "wedge" is conceived as an object in the auditorium space and creates the acoustic vestibule between the auditorium and the lobby.

37 | GALERIA SEQUIERA, BRAGA, PORTUGAL, 1998–2001

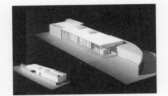

172 | 173

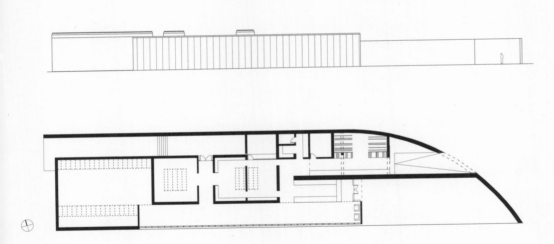

This 7,000-square-foot building will house a commercial gallery on a sloping site that includes an early-twentieth-century villa, a renovated four-hundred-year-old stone farm complex, an underground art storage building, and renovated orchards and vineyards. The dimensional module of the gallery is determined by the unique granite post trellises that support the grapes. An existing stone wall is rebuilt and extended to form the upper wall of the building.

38|MUSEO PICASSO MALAGA, MALAGA, SPAIN, 1998–2001

174|175

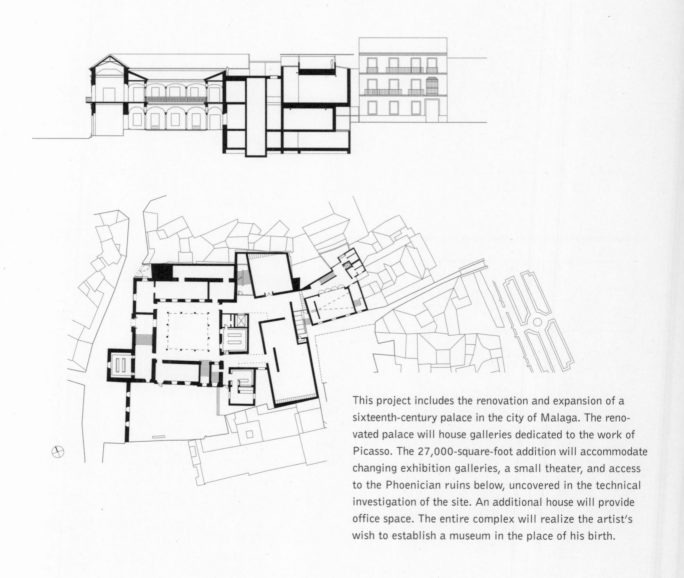

This project includes the renovation and expansion of a sixteenth-century palace in the city of Malaga. The renovated palace will house galleries dedicated to the work of Picasso. The 27,000-square-foot addition will accommodate changing exhibition galleries, a small theater, and access to the Phoenician ruins below, uncovered in the technical investigation of the site. An additional house will provide office space. The entire complex will realize the artist's wish to establish a museum in the place of his birth.

AWARDS

Honor Award, 1999, American Institute of Architects, New York Chapter, Acadia Summer Arts Program, Mount Desert, Maine.

Business Week/Architectural Record Award, 1999, Helmut Lang Boutique, New York, New York

Design Distinction Award, 1998, I.D. Magazine, Helmut Lang Boutique, New York, New York.

Honorable Mention, 1998, XI Bienal de Arquitectura de Quito, Andy Warhol Museum, Pittsburgh, Pennsylvania.

Interiors Award, 1997, American Institute of Architects, New York Chapter, Paula Cooper Gallery, New York, New York.

Citation, 1997, Architecture, Progressive Architecture Awards, Matchbox House, Orient, New York.

Dean's Outstanding Alumni Award, 1996, School of Architecture, Syracuse University.

Record Award, 1996, Architectural Record, House for an Artist and a Writer, Cape Breton, Nova Scotia.

Record Award, 1994, Architectural Record, Andy Warhol Museum, Pittsburgh, Pennsylvania.

Gold Award, 1992, I.D. Magazine, Gagosian Gallery, New York, New York.

Honor Award, 1988, American Institute of Architects, New York Chapter, Dia Center for the Arts, 548 West Twenty-second Street, New York, New York.

Citation, 1988, International Association of Lighting Designers for the Dia Center for the Arts, 548 West Twenty-second Street, New York, New York.

BIOGRAPHY

1947   Born in Buffalo, New York

1965   Entered Syracuse University

1967   Awarded fellowship for travel in Europe

1968   Designed and built Gluckman Residence working as carpenter's assistant to the general contractor

1969   Worked part time for Werner Seligmann

1970   Worked part time for Skoler/Lee Partnership

1971   Graduated Syracuse University School of Architecture

1972–75 Worked for Stahl/Bennett Architects, Boston

1975–76 Sailed a small boat from Scotland to Cape Town to Rio de Janeiro. Traveled through Southern Africa and South America and came to New York to do design/ build with college roommate Frederick Stelle.

1977   Established office of Frederick Stelle/Richard Gluckman Architects, New York

1985   Established office of Richard Gluckman Architects, New York

1989   Invited by Rafael Moneo to be a visiting critic at the Harvard University Graduate School of Design

1990   Symposium Panelist, "New Museum Architecture and Contemporary Art," Des Moines, Iowa

1994   Invited by Rem Koolhaas to participate in the final submission for the Tate Bankside Competition

1995   Charette participant: "The Pension Building/The National Building Museum," GSA, National Endowment for the Arts

1995   Visiting Critic at the Harvard University Graduate School of Design, teaching jointly with Jane Wernick of Ove Arup & Partners on architecture and technology

1996   Joined the board of directors of The Andy Warhol Foundation for the Visual Arts

1997   Sargent Visiting Professor of Architecture, Syracuse University

1998   Established office of Gluckman Mayner Architects, New York

1998   Joined the board of directors of the Van Alen Institute

1998   Named Fellow of the American Institute of Architects

1998–99 Jury Member, International Design Competition for The Center for Contemporary Arts, Rome

1998   Selected as architects for The Austin Museum of Art

1999   Selected as architects for the North Carolina Museum of Art

BIBLIOGRAPHY

BOOKS

Angell, Callie, ed. The Andy Warhol Museum. Stuttgart: Cantz, 1994.

Davis, Douglas. The Museum Transformed. New York: Abbeville Press, 1990.

Henderson, Justin. Museum Architecture. Gloucester, Mass.: Rockport, 1998.

Newhouse, Victoria. Towards a New Museum. New York: The Monacelli Press, 1998.

Vercelloni, Matteo. New Showrooms and Art Galleries in USA. Milan: Edizioni L'Archivolto, 1999.

Vercelloni, Matteo. Urban Interior in New York and USA. Milan: Edizioni L'Archivolto, 1996.

Wang, Wilfred, and Annette Becker, eds. Architektur Jahrbuch/Architecture in Germany.
    Munich: Prestel, 1998.

ARTICLES

"1998 Cultural Diary." Interior Design, December 1998, 128.

Abercrombie, Stanley. "Richard Gluckman." Interior Design, May 1995, 140–43

Adams, Brooks. "Art World Diva." Elle Décor, February/March 1997, 128–33.

Adams, Brooks. "Industrial Strength Warhol." Art in America, September 1994, 71–77.

Antoniades, Anthony C. "The Art Spaces of Richard Gluckman." The World of Buildings, December 1998,
    78–96.

Balint, Juliana. "Minimalismo ad Arte." Case da Abitare, November 1998, 62–67.

Barreneche, Raul A. "Building a Specialty in Art." Architecture, November 1996, 157, 164–67.

Bussel, Abby. "Lite Brite." Interior Design, April 1999.

Colacello, Bob. "Remains of the Dia." Vanity Fair, September 1996, 73+.

Colman, David. "Art & Architecture." Elle Décor, December 1997, 183–88.

Dillon, David. "Playing the Competitions Game." Architectural Record, November 1997, 62–67.

Dillon, David. "The Georgia O'Keeffe Museum." Architectural Record, January 1998, 80–85.

Frieman, Ziva. "Reinventing the Ranch." Metropolitan Home, October 1997, 80–86.

Ganem, Mark. "O'Keeffe." W, June 1997, 194–97.

Geibel, Victoria. "Undesigned." Art & Auction, July/August 1990, 53–56.

Giovannini, Joseph. "Fort Worth's New Museum." Architecture, June 1997, 44–45.

Giovannini, Joseph. "The Whitney's Modest Expansion." Art in America, September 1998, 31.

Gluckman, Richard. "Architect's Statement." In **The Andy Warhol Museum**, 53–56. New York: D.A.P., 1994.

Gluckman, Richard. "The Warhol Museum, Pittsburgh." **9H** 9, 268–73.

Glueck, Grace. "Dia Foundation, Back from the Brink." **New York Times**, October 7, 1987, C23.

Gurewitsch, Matthew. "Met Tour No. 4." **Town & Country**, May 1995, 83.

Hoban, Phoebe. "Ultra, Nana and Tama Go to Pittsburgh: A Warholian 'Wow' Greets Maos, Cows."
    New York Observer, May 23, 1994, 1, 17.

Kastner, Jeffrey. "Portfolio Management." **Art News**, January 1999, 46.

Karmel, Pepe. "Ross Bleckner." **New York Times**, May 10, 1996, C23.

Kellogg, Craig. "Plain Canvas." **Wallpaper**, September/October 1997, 56–57.

Kreger, Leah. "Points of Departure: A review of the Andy Warhol Museum." **9H** 9, 266–67.

Lowry Patricia. "Designing the Andy Warhol Museum." **Carnegie Magazine**,
    May/June 1994, 32–37.

"Matchbox House", **Architecture** (Annual Awards Issue), January 1997, 90–91.

Merkel, Jayne. "The New Minimalism." **Oculus**, January 1997, 7–9.

Merkel, Jayne, and Victoria Reed. "Seattle through Eastern and Western Eyes." **Oculus**,
    May 1996, 14–15.

Merkel, Jayne, and Victoria Reed. "OMA with Richard Gluckman." **Architecture New York** 13, 1996, 40–44.

Muschamp, Herbert. "The Theatrical Premiere of a Fantasy by Koolhaas." **New York Times**, April 8, 1999,
    B1, B5.

Pearson, Cliford A.. "Rural Icon Dares to be Simple." **Architectural Record**, April 1996, 102–5.

Pittel, Christine. "Alchemist of Light." **Harper's Bazaar**, January 1993, 94–99.

Quigg, Joe. "Andy Steals the Show." **Tate, the Art Magazine**, Summer 1994, 6.

Quigg, Joe. "Richard Gluckman Architects." **Architectural Design**, June/July 1994, 66–69.

Rimanelli, David. "Chelsea Passage." **Interior Design**, September 1997, 172–77.

Rus, Mayer. "Space Craft." **Interior Design**, September 1991, 222–25.

Schwartzman, Alan. "Expanding an Icon." **Architecture**, June 1998, 108–13.

Searing, Helen. "The Brillo Box in the Warehouse: Museums of Contemporary Art and Industrial
    Conversions." In **The Andy Warhol Museum**, 39–65. New York: D.A.P., 1994.

Smith, Roberta. "Art: Beuys, Palermo and Knoebel at the New Dia." **New York Times**,
    October 9, 1987, C36.

Smith, Roberta. "Whitney Whittles Intimate Corners." **New York Times**, April 3, 1998, E35–39.

Stein, Karen. "Home Again." **Architectural Record**, September, 1994, 74–79.

Stein, Karen. "Outside In." **New York**, October 9, 1995, 37–57.

Stevens, Mark. "Let the Sun Shine In." **New York**, April 6, 1998, 44–47.

Thompson, Helen. "Desert Blooms." **Metropolitan Home**, July/August 1997, 43–43.

Vincent, Steven. "The Art World's Architect." **Art and Auction**, November 1996, 90–92.

Von Rezzori, Gregor. "A Personal Palette." **House and Garden**, June 1993, 104–10, 182.

Webster, Peter. "Ten Trends." **Departures**, March/April 1999, 42.

Wright, George. "A Modern Neighbor for the Kimbell: The Modern Art Museum of Fort Worth Competition."
    Competitions, Spring 1998, 28–39.

ACKNOWLEDGMENTS

A book is not a building. A book attempts, with two-dimensional images and text, to relate the process of thinking, making, and experiencing a building. I am extremely wary of the ability of images and text to relate this process.

To the degree that this is successful, great credit goes to Michael Rock and Aline Ozkan at 2 x 4. I also acknowledge Catherine Dunn for her invaluable assistance. I am happy for the opportunity given to me by Gianfranco Monacelli and for the efforts of Andrea Monfried and Ron Broadhurst to bring the book to completion. I am amazed by and grateful to Hal Foster for his essay here and for years of patient explanations to an intellectual neophyte.

A career is impossible to predict. I did not set out to become a museum architect or a renovation architect. I wanted to be an architect. Since I was ten years old when I was told the definition of the word.

My grandfather trained as an architect and introduced me to drawing and to his workshop. My parents provided me with unqualified support and the extraordinary gift of their own house. It was this experience that gave me the confidence and desire to be my own boss.

The builders, to whom we are inextricably linked, have earned my respect and gratitude, especially Jim Scheuefele, who has been a quiet collaborator.

Our clients have provided the challenge, the money, and, occasionally, the insight to enable us to realize our best projects.

My employees and students over the years have probably given me more than I have given them.

The artists have provided insight, vision, support, and constant surprise and wonder; especially Dan Flavin and Richard Serra, two of the best architects I know.

Bruce Fowle provided support and advice from the beginning.

Heiner Friedrich introduced me to an extraordinary realm of art.

Charlie Wright allowed me to continue to explore this realm.

Carmen Jimenez, my co-conspirator in things museological.

My first partner, Frederick Stelle, was the perfect complement and a great friend.

My second partner, David Mayner, is the foundation upon which the office rests. I cannot express well enough my gratitude for his loyalty, hard work, dedicated professionalism, and penetrating insight into a difficult business and a great profession.

The support, love, and wisdom of my children, Nell and Marina, and my wife, Tiffany Bell, are the foundation upon which I rest.

EMPLOYEE LIST 1979–1999

Gabrielle Adelphin	Zazu Faure	Monique Mason	**Nina Seirafi**
David Adler	**Mark Fiedler**	**David Mayner**	**Michael Sheridan**
Katrin Ashbury	Dennis Gibbons	Michael McClure	Anja Simons
John Averitt	Frances Goodwin	Connie Marie McGlon	Michael Simpson
Timothy Bade	Patricia Gora	Jane McNichol	James Slade
Deborah Barlow	Matthew Gottsegen	Michael Meredith	Suzanne Song
Andrew Bartle	Ernest Guenzburger	Tom Miller	**Jane Stageberg**
George Beckwith	**Michael Hamilton**	Manuel Morales	Michelle Stark
David Bers	Robert Han	Brad Nettle	Stanley Stinnett
Raffaella Bortoluzzi	David Hanawalt	Talya Nevo-Hacochen	Douglas Suisman
Eileen Blair Bosman	Richard Hayes	Patrick O'Brien	**David Taber**
Jonathan Bowser	Mark Heckler	Amy O'Neill	**Ching Tai**
Louise Braverman	Rebecca Henn	William O'Neill	**Dana Tang**
Jennifer Brayer	Daniel Heyden	Jon Pachuta	**Brett Tipert**
Alexis Briski	Caroline Holliday	Antonio Palladino	Kathy Titus
Sean Briski	**Alex Hurst**	**Russo Panduro**	**William Truitt**
Samuel Brown	Ivan Ilyashov	**Iona Park**	Michele Tung
Alan Bruton	Philip Ivory	Rodman Paul, Jr.	Peggy Walker
Elena Cannon	Sara Jacobs	Paul Pelletier	Loren Weeks
Celia Chang	**Srdjan Jovanovic Weiss**	Diane Pettit	Scott Weinkle
Eric Chang	Niels Kampmann	Andrea Popa	Hali Weiss
Wilmay Choy	Sheila Kavanagh	Ray Porfilio	**Perry Whidden**
Judy Chung	**Andrea Keiner**	**David Pysh**	**Robert White**
Lea Ciavarra	Diana Kellogg	Michael Regan	Deborah Wolinsky
Melissa Cicetti	Billy Kimball	Mar Reventos	**Gregory Yang**
Jim Clark	David King	**Elizabeth Rexrode**	Jimmie Yoo
Susan Cleary	Leah Kreger	Alex Riccobono	**Dean Young**
Dominick Cock	John Lamonica	Lise Roberts	Andy Zago
Ethan Cohen	Lynette Lanier	**Danny Roldan**	Dolores Zago
Chris Collir	Gregg Latchow	Ann Rolland	
Robin Corsino-Pena	Elizabeth Lacey	Rob Rothblatt	
Jennifer Crawley	Richard Lavenstein	Kristin Royer	
John DiGregorio	Steven Learner	Margot Ruckstein	
Pier Djerejian	James Leet	Orla Ryan	
James Doerfler	Amy Lelyveld	David Saik	
Joshua Dudley	En-Chuan Liu	Michael Samuels	
Catherine Dunn	Robert Lombard	Eric Santiago	
Sarah Dunn	Taylor Louden	Ira Schachner	
Joan Eckstein	Patricia Malcolm	Christophen Scholz	
Tamara Embrey	**Martin Marciano**	Zinta Schnore	
James Esseks	Dee Martin	Donna Seftel	
Mary Faithorn	**Leo Mascotte**	Annabelle Selldorf	

Denotes current employee

PROJECT LIST* 1968–1999

RICHARD GLUCKMAN DESIGNER

1968 Gluckman Residence, Glenwood, New York
1969 Divis Residence, Fire Island, New York
1971 Clark Camp, Big Moose Lake, New York

FREDERICK STELLE
RICHARD GLUCKMAN ARCHITECTS

1976 Doyle Residence, Franklin Lakes, New Jersey
     Stelle Residence, Mt. Kisco, New York
1977 Friedrich/de Menil Residence, New York, New York
1978 Langley Studio, New York, New York
     Schmidt Residence, New York, New York
     Stern Residence, New York, New York
     Weisenbach/Stuen Residence, New York, New York
1978–80 Dia, Various Installations, New York, New York
1979 Dia, **The New York Earth Room** by Walter de Maria, New York, New York
     Ho Residence and Studio, New York, New York
     Dia Office Building (Project), New York, New York
     Dia, Dan Flavin Installation, Pedestrian Tunnel (Project), New York, New York
     Dia, Dan Flavin Installation, World Trade Center (Project), New York, New York
     Dia, Dan Flavin, Dick's Castle (Project), Garrison, New York
     Janelle Residence, New York, New York
     Mabon Residence, New York, New York
     Moeller Residence, New York, New York
     Noble/Blagden Residence, New York, New York
     Pondview Apartments, Middletown, Connecticut
     Ruben Residence, Poquott, New York
1980 Dia, **The Broken Kilometer** by Walter de Maria, New York, New York
     Dia, Office Building, New York, New York
     Dia, Robert Whitman Building, New York, New York
     Dia, Dan Flavin Installation, Anchorage, Alaska, Federal Building
     Kuhn Residence, New York, New York
     Langley Soundstage, New York, New York
     The Pastures (Project), Albany, New York
     Robinson Square Mall (Project), Albany, New York
     Brookside Apartments (Project), Middletown, Connecticut
     Dia, Dan Flavin Art Institute, Bridgehampton, New York
     Shirk Residence Addition, Chicago, Illinois
1981 527 Madison Avenue (Project), New York, New York
     Plaza 49 (Project), New York, New York
     Botzow Residence, Bedford, New York
1982 Barnard Residence, New York, New York
1982–85 David's Cookies Stores (50), Various locations in the United States and Japan
     Liederman Residence, New York, New York
     Manhattan Market, New York, New York
     Pemex Office Building (Project), New York, New York
     Pettit Residence, New York, New York
     Siplon Residence, New York, New York
     Welles Residence, New York, New York
1983–85 Sedutto's Ice Cream Stores (6), Various locations in the New York metropolitan area
1983 Burack/Weiss Residence, New York, New York
     Freylinghuysen Residence, New York, New York
     Gordon Residence, Southold, New York
     Kleiman Residence, New York, New York
     Overlock Residence, New York, New York

1983 Farragut Shelter, Saint-Gaudens National Historic Site, Cornish, New Hampshire
     Thyssen/Bornemisza Residence (in association with Renzo Mongiardino), New York, New York
1984 Golkin Residence and Studio, New York, New York
     Le Boutellier Residence, Bridgehampton, New York
     Huggins Residence, New York, New York
     Keller Residence, Wainscott, New York
     Lott/Divis Residence, Oakdale, New York
     Ruth Residence, New York, New York
     Sayles Residence, New York, New York
     Zeigler Residence, New York, New York

RICHARD GLUCKMAN ARCHITECTS

1985 Brooke Alexander Gallery (in association with Max Gordon), New York, New York
     Hughes Residence, New York, New York
     Miller Residence, New York, New York
     Niarchos Residence (in association with Renzo Mongiardino), New York, New York
     Mass Moca Submission (Project), North Adams, Massachusetts
     Pozzi Residence, New York, New York
     Richardson Residence, Jamestown Island, Rhode Island
     Maeght Lelong Gallery (in association with Max Gordon), New York, New York
     Murray/Holman Residence (in association with Max Gordon), New York, New York
     Ferry Residence (in association with Max Gordon), New York, New York
     Pilmar Residence, New York, New York
     Paula Cooper Gallery (in association with Max Gordon), New York, New York
     Marshall Residence, New York, New York
     Hartheimer/Golding Residence, New York, New York
     Robert Miller Gallery, New York, New York
     Bartlett/Carriere Residence (in association with Max Gordon), New York, New York
     Schlinkert Residence, Brooklyn, New York
1986 Shapiro/Phelan Loft (in association with Max Gordon), New York, New York
     Farideh Cadot Gallery, New York, New York
     Dia Center for the Arts, New York, New York
     Gressel Residence, New York, New York
     Caine Residence, New York, New York
     Bell Residence, Cheston-on-Wye, Maryland
     Wright Residence, New York, New York
     Keller Residence, New York, New York
     Galerie St. Etienne, New York, New York
     Marschner Residence (in association with Max Gordon), New York, New York
     Lumet Residence (Project), New York, New York
     Moeller/Bucholtz Residence (Project), Middletown, New York
     Livingston Residence, New York, New York
     Carter Lawson Residence, New York, New York
1987 Kallir Residence, New York, New York
     Peter Brams, Inc., Offices, New York, New York
     Wright Residence, New York, New York
     Read Residence, New York, New York
     Read Residence, Bellport, Long Island
     Frank Residence, New York, New York
     Caine/Gressel/Midgley/Slater Offices, New York, New York
1987 Lelyveld Residence, New York, New York

1987 Garner Tullis Workshop, New York, New York
Di Blasi Residence, New York, New York
I.C.I. Offices, New York, New York
Massimo Audiello Gallery, New York, New York
International With Monument (in association with
    Max Gordon), New York, New York
Brickell Residence, New York, New York
Pamela Auchincloss Gallery, New York, New York
Merrin Residence, New York, New York
Brody Residence (in association with Max Gordon),
    New York, New York
Donald Baechler Residence, New York, New York
1988 Salvatore Ala Gallery, New York, New York
Wagner/Ryman Residence, New York, New York
Ryman Studio, New York, New York
Frelinghuysen Residence, New York, New York
Serra Residence (in association with Max Gordon),
    New York, New York
John Good Gallery, New York, New York
Pat Hearn Gallery, New York, New York
Kenney Residence, New York, New York
Paula Cooper 2, New York, New York
Gorovoy Residence (Project), New York, New York
Divis Residence II, Fire Island, New York
Barbara Flynn Gallery, New York, New York
Loeb Residence, New York, New York
McGough Residence, East Marion, New York
Sherman/Heiss Loft, New York, New York
Chanin Building Lobby Renovation, New York, New York
Reed/Ball Residence, New York, New York
Brooke Alexander Print Gallery, New York, New York
1989 Stein/Gladstone Gallery, New York, New York
Swistel Residence, New York, New York
Rubell Residence Library, New York, New York
Chase Residence, New York, New York
Christine Burgin Gallery, New York, New York
Clemente Residence, New York, New York
Renovation, Boston Museum of Fine Arts, Boston,
    Massachusetts
Vrej Baghoomian Gallery, New York, New York
Cunningham Residence, New York, New York
Printed Matter, New York, New York
White Street Studios, New York, New York
Yamakoshi Art/ Nobart Gallery (Project),
    New York, New York
The Andy Warhol Museum, Pittsburgh, Pennsylvania
S. Bitter-Larkin Gallery Inc., New York, New York
Nina Freudenheim Gallery I, Buffalo, New York
Petersburg Press, New York, New York
Vrej Baghoomian Gallery, New York, New York
Row Residence, Cushing Island, Maine
Kouri Residence, New York, New York
Gordon Residence II, Southold, New York
David Salle Residence and Studio, Crested Butte, Colorado
David McKee Gallery, New York, New York
Drayton Residence, Valley Forge, Pennsylvania
Freudenheim Gallery II, Buffalo, New York
Turrell Installation Repair at PS1, Queens, New York
Turrell Installation, Stein-Gladstone Gallery,
    New York, New York
1990 Robert Ryman Pavilion, Pharmakon '90, Tokyo, Japan
James Turrell Installation, Stein-Gladstone Gallery,
    New York, New York,
    Kouri Residence, Pool Structure (Project),
    Greenwich, Connecticut

1990 Rubin/Spangle Gallery, New York, New York
Meyer Vaisman Residence (Project), New York, New York
Serra Studio, New York, New York
Dia Center for the Arts, New York, New York
Barbara Gladstone Gallery, New York, New York
Gagosian Gallery (Project), New York, New York
Fundacion San German, San German, Puerto Rico
Laura Carpenter Gallery, Sante Fe, New Mexico
Yasuda/Murray Residence , New York, New York
Gordon Residence, New York, New York
Blum Helman Gallery (Project), New York, New York
142 Greene Street Lobby, New York, New York
Bing & Migs Wright Residence,
    New York, New York
1991 Ryman/Wagner Residence, New York, New York
Questrom Residence Addition (Project), Greenwich,
    Connecticut
John Baldessari Residence (Project), New York, New York
Gallery St. Etienne, New York, New York
Marlborough Gallery, New York, New York
Jason Rubell Gallery, Palm Beach, Florida
Menschel Residence Addition (Project), Nantucket,
    Massachusetts
Akira Ikeda Gallery (Project), New York, New York
Gagosian Gallery, New York, New York
Mary Boone Gallery, New York, New York
Atarazanas: Centro de Arte Contemporaneo (Project),
    Seville, Spain
Marlborough Gallery, Madrid, Spain
Pabellon Mudeja, Seville, Spain
Palacio Episcopal, Malaga, Spain
GAP Exhibition Space, San Francisco, California
1992 Whitney Museum of American Art, Lobby,
    New York, New York,
Levine Residence, New York, New York
Paula Cooper Gallery, New York, New York
Marshall Residence, New York, New York
88 Central Park West Lobby Renovation, New York,
    New York
Murray/Holman Residence, New York, New York
Fundacion Jorge Castillo (Project), Santiago de
    Campostela, Spain
Dia Center 545 I (Project), New York, New York
Galerie Kaj Forsblom, Zurich, Switzerland
David Gressel CFX, New York, New York
Jason Rubell Gallery, Miami Beach, Florida
Dia Center 535 (Project), New York, New York
Dia-Beuys Installation, 7000 Oaks, New York, New York
Dia Center Offices, New York, New York
Juan Usle Residence, New York, New York
Industrial Commercial Bank of China, Shanghai, China
    (Joint venture; Fox & Fowle, Gluckman & Liu)
Tony Shafrazi Gallery, New York, New York
Merrin Residence, New York, New York
1993 Elli Kouri Residence, New York, New York
South Central First City (Project), Wuhan, China
    (Joint venture; Fox & Fowle, Gluckman & Liu)
Charles and Barbara Wright Residence, New York, New York
Anthony D'Offay Gallery, London, England
Kouri Capitol Group, New York, New York
Andy Warhol Foundation for the Visual Arts,
    New York, New York
Paula Cooper Gallery, New York, New York
Lloyd Residence, New York, New York

1993 Shenhua Commercial Building, Shanghai, China
     (Joint venture; Fox & Fowle, Gluckman & Liu)
1994 House for an Artist and a Writer, Cape Breton, Nova Scotia
     Donald Fisher Gallery (Project), Atherton, California
     Richard Avedon Exhibition, Whitney Museum of American
        Art, New York, New York
     Joseph Stella Exhibition, Whitney Museum of American Art,
        New York, New York
     Lustmord, Jenny Holzer Installation, Barbara Gladstone
        Gallery, New York, New York
     Jenny Holzer Installation, Wiesbaden, Germany
     Jenny Holzer Installation, Erlauf, Austria
     Scaife Galleries, MOA, Carnegie Institute,
        Pittsburgh, Pennsylvania
     Charles and Barbara Wright Residence, Seattle, Washington
     Serra, Duane Street, New York, New York
     Berlin Holocaust Memorial Competition,
        with Richard Serra (Project), Berlin, Germany
     American Center Exhibition Space, Paris, France
     Dia Cafe, New York, New York
     Whitney Facilities, New York, New York
     Jenny Holzer, Peace Garden (Project), Sogetsu Plaza,
        Sogetsu Kaikan, Japan
     Tony Shafrazi Gallery, New York, New York
     Site Santa Fe, Santa Fe, New Mexico
     Richard Brothers Residence (Project),
        Orcas Island, Washington
     Whitney Museum of American Art, New York, New York
     Ryman/Wagner Residence, New York, New York
     Williams Residence, New York, New York
     Tate Gallery-Bankside (Project) with Rem Koolhaas,
        London, England
     Merrin Residence, Mt. Kisco, New York
1995 Ethan Ryman Residence, New York, New York
     Brancusi Exhibition, Philadelphia Museum of Art,
        Philadelphia, Pennsylvania
     Matchbox House, Orient, New York
     Cordy Ryman Residence, New York, New York
     Brooke Alexander Gallery, New York, New York
     Formica/Heimstra Residence, Orient, New York
     Wayfinding and Public Amenities, Carnegie Institute,
        Pittsburgh, Pennsylvania
     Burden/Warren Residence, Portland, Oregon
     Lee/Lies Residence, Tesque, New Mexico
     Brubach Residence, New York, New York
     Pool Structure, Cape Breton, Nova Scotia
     Limpe Residence, New York, New York
     Dance Cafe (Project), New York, New York
     Paula Cooper Gallery, New York, New York
1996 Mary Boone Gallery, New York, New York
     Row Residence, Cushing Island, Maine
     Foster/Tait Residence, New York, New York
     "Japanese Prints" Exhibition, MOA, Carnegie
        Institute, Pittsburgh, Pennsylvania
     Cezanne Exhibition, Philadelphia Museum of Art,
        Philadelphia, Pennsylvania
     The Schoolhouse, ASAP (Project), Mt. Desert, Maine
     Pittsburgh Cultural Trust, with Robert Wilson,
        Pittsburgh, Pennsylvania
     Fabric Workshop, Philadelphia, Pennsylvania
     Dia 548-Sandback Installation, New York, New York
     Artist's Studio, ASAP, Mt. Desert, Maine
     Keith and Kathy Sachs Residence, Rydal, Pennsylvania
     Georgia O'Keeffe Museum, Sante Fe, New Mexico
     Site Sante Fe 1996, Sante Fe, New Mexico

1996 Dia Center 545 II, New York, New York
     Modern Art Museum (Competition), Fort Worth, Texas,
     Second Stage Theatre, with Rem Koolhaas,
        New York, New York
     Mori Art Center (in association with KPF, JPI), Tokyo, Japan
     Versace Boutique, New York, New York
     Pinault Residence (Project), New York, New York
     Ross Residence, New York, New York
1997 Deutsche Guggenheim Berlin, Berlin, Germany
     Krauss/Hollier Residence, New York, New York
     Versace-Chevy Chase (Project), Chevy Chase, Maryland
     Versace-Prototype (Project),
     Versace-Chicago (Project), Chicago, Illinois
     Versace-South Beach (Project), Miami, Florida
     Acoustiguide
     Rosenfeld Residence, New York, New York
     Neiman Marcus Beechwood, Cleveland, Ohio
     Neiman Marcus Biltmore, Phoenix, Arizona
     Neiman Marcus Seattle, Seattle, Washington
     Warhol Fashion Show, Whitney Museum of
        American Art, New York, New York
     Helmut Lang Boutique, New York, New York
     Gambaccini Residence, New York, New York
     Cheim & Read Gallery, New York, New York
     Luhring Augustine Gallery, New York, New York
     Andrea Rosen Gallery, New York, New York
     CFX, New York, New York
     Contemporary Galleries Renovation (Project),
        Philadelphia Museum of Art, Philadelphia, Pennsylvania
     Gianni Versace Exhibit, Metropolitan Museum of Art,
        New York, New York
     United Methodist Church (Project), Bronx, New York
     Wright Gallery, Seattle, Washington
     Watermill Center, Watermill, New York
     Boesky Residence, New York, New York
     Carnegie-Normandie Panels, Carnegie Institute,
        Pittsburgh, Pennsylvania

GLUCKMAN MAYNER ARCHITECTS

1998 Museo Picasso Malaga, Malaga, Spain
     Helmut Lang Basement, New York, New York
     Sotheby's Penthouse, New York, New York
     Diego Cortez Residence (Project), New York, New York
     Roy Lichtenstein Plaza (Project), Singapore, Malaysia
     Helmut Lang Residence (Project), New York, New York
     The Spa at Enchantment (Project), Sedona, Arizona
     Galeria Sequiera (Project), Braga, Portugal
     Helmut Lang Offices and Showroom, New York, New York
     Yves Saint Laurent Boutique, New York, New York
     Robert Ryman Studio, New York, New York
     Georgia O'Keeffe Study Center, Santa Fe, New Mexico
     Katayone Adele Boutique, New York, New York
     Sandy Brant Residence, New York, New York
     Austin Museum of Art (Project), Austin, Texas
1999 North Carolina Museum of Art (Project), Raleigh,
        North Carolina
     Gordon Residence III, (Project), Southold, New York
     Oeri/Bodenmann Residence, (Project), New York, New York
     Gap Exhibition II, (Project), San Francisco, California
     Gagosian Gallery, (Project), New York, New York

ARTIST CREDITS

THE NEW YORK EARTH ROOM
Walter de Maria, **The New York Earth Room**, 1977.
Dia Center for the Arts location at 141 Wooster Street,
New York, NY 10012. ©Dia Center for the Arts 1997.

THE BROKEN KILOMETER
Walter de Maria, **The Broken Kilometer**, 1979.
Dia Art Foundation Location 393 West Broadway, New York,
New York 10012. ©Dia Art Foundation 1980.

DIA CENTER FOR THE ARTS (DIA 548)
Joseph Beuys, Drawing Installation and Installation view of
Double Fond, **Fond IV/4** and **Fond III/3**, October 9, 1987–June
19, 1988.

Imi Knoebel, **Room 19**, October 9, 1987–June 19, 1988.

Blinky Palermo, **To the People of New York City**, October 9,
1987–June 19, 1988.

Robert Ryman, Installation at the Dia in 1989.

FRIEDRICH/DE MENIL RESIDENCE
Dan Flavin, Installation on floor and ceiling.

GAGOSIAN GALLERY
Richard Serra, **Two Forged Rounds (for Buster Keaton)**, 1991,
installation for Gagosian Gallery. Forged weatherproof steel,
each round 64" high, 88½" diameter. Collection: Robert and Jane
Meyerhoff, Phoenix, Maryland. ©Dia Center for the Arts 1997.

Richard Serra, **Intersection II**, 1992–93, installation at
Gagosian Gallery. Weatherproof steel, four conical sections,
each 13'1½" x 55'3⅜" x 2⅛", overall 13'1½" x 55'9⅜" x 24'.
Private collection, promised gift to the Museum of Modern
Art, New York. © Dia Art Foundation.

LUSTMORD
Jenny Holzer, **Lustmord** shown at Barbara Gladstone Gallery,
New York, 1994.

DIA 545 II
Richard Serra, installation of three **Torqued Ellipses** at Dia
Center for the Arts, New York, 1997. Collection: Dia Center
for the Arts, New York. Gift of Leonard and Louise Riggio.

MARY BOONE GALLERY
Ross Bleckner, installation at Mary Boone Gallery,
New York, May 1996.

PAULA COOPER GALLERY
Tony Smith, **Moondog**, installation at Paula Cooper Gallery,
© 1999 Estate of Tony Smith/Artists Rights Society (ARS),
New York.

The Carl Andre works are identified from left to right as follows:

Angelarc, New York, 1995. Poplar, 37 units, 2" x 10" x 50"
(5.08 x 25.4 x 127 cm) each; 2" x 239.5" (5.08 x 608.33 x
825.5 cm) overall (CA-255-SC).

Slit, New York, 1981. Steel and copper, 38 units of steel,
19 units of copper, ³/₁₇" x 40½" x 31'2" (.5 x 103 x 950 cm)
overall (CA-173-SC).

81 CuFe (The Net of Hephaestus), New York, 1981. Copper
and steel, (81-unit square), ³/₁₆" x 20" x 20" (.5 x 50 x 50 cm)
each; ³/₁₆" x 180" x 180" (.5 x 457.2 x 457.2 cm) overall
(CA-122-SC).

HELMUT LANG BOUTIQUE
Jenny Holzer, Installation for Helmut Lang, installation at
Helmut Lang Boutique.

ANDY WARHOL MUSEUM
All artwork by Andy Warhol. All photos are courtesy of
The Andy Warhol Museum.
Warhol Café with **Marilyn Monroe** prints, 1967.
Elvis (Eleven Times), ca. 1963.
Vote McGovern, 1972, and **Mao** portraits, 1972–73, on **Mao**
wallpaper, 1974.
Skull paintings, 1976.
Shadows, 1978, installation.

GEORGIA O'KEEFFE MUSEUM
Jimson Weed, Georgia O'Keeffe
From a Day with Juan, Georgia O'Keeffe

PHOTOGRAPHY CREDITS

Cover (Gagosian Gallery): Edward Hueber
The New York Earthroom: John Cliett for the Dia Foundation
The Broken Kilometer: Jon Abbott for the Dia Foundation
Dia Center for the Arts 548: Noel Allum/Dan Cornish
The Andy Warhol Museum: Paul Rocheleau
Wright Residence: Dan Cornish for Esto
Gordon Residence: Paul Warchol
Row Residence: Paul Warchol
Gagosian Gallery: Edward Hueber
Dia 545 I: Jock Pottle
The Warhol Foundation for the Visual Arts: Edward Hueber
House for an Artist and a Writer: James Steeves
Whitney Museum of American Art: Paul Warchol
Matchbox House: Jock Pottle
Mary Boone Gallery: Zindeman/Fremont, Paul Warchol
Paula Cooper Gallery: Lydia Gould
Versace Boutique, New York: Lydia Gould
Versace Building, South Beach: Jock Pottle
Modern Art Museum, Fort Worth: Jock Pottle
Acadia Summer Arts Program: Paul Warchol
Georgia O'Keeffe Museum: Robert Reck
Dia 545 II: Lydia Gould
Galeria Sequiera: Jock Pottle
Second Stage Theater: Tom Powell
Museo Picasso Malaga: Jock Pottle